CIVIL WAR BURIALS IN BALTIMORE'S LOUDON PARK CEMETERY

BY *ANNA MILLER WATRING*

CLEARFIELD

Printed for
Clearfield Company, Inc. by
Genealogical Publishing Co., Inc.
Baltimore, Maryland
1996

International Standard Book Number: 0-8063-4620-5

Made in the United States of America

INTRODUCTION

Founded in 1853, Loudon Park Cemetery is one of the largest in the world. Always accessible, it was on the main line of the Pennsylvania Railroad between Baltimore and Washington and for a time boasted its own funeral car, a regular service of the city trolley line. Loudon Park is the final resting place for many famous people and almost every family in Baltimore has a relative buried there.

The 1850s ended with a decrease in burials at Loudon Park. As a result of the Civil War, the coming decade would see a great increase in the population. 2,300 Union soldiers and at least 650 Confederate soldiers would be buried there.

During the Civil War the government purchased a section for the Union Army. This became known as the Government Lot. In 1903 the federal government purchased a larger section which included most of the Union burial plots. Other Union soldiers were eventually moved there. This portion is now operated separately as Loudon National Cemetery.

The first Confederate soldiers were buried in May 1862 in plots thought to have been donated by lot holders sympathetic to the Southern cause. Later, the cemetery traded lots with those deed-holders and buried all the Confederate soldiers in one section. This area became famous as Confederate Hill. There are 650 known graves. The last burial, in August 1937, was that of Col. Hobart Aisquith, aged 92, of the 1st. Md. Cavalry. However, not all Confederate soldiers in Loudon Park are buried on Confederate Hill. In a corner of Loudon National Cemetery a stone monument, erected by the U. S. Government, marks the resting place of 29 Confederate soldiers who died at Ft. McHenry while prisoners of war, and of three camp followers.

The data contained within this book were hand-copied around 1981 from the original Loudon Park interment books by Robert W. Barnes. The whereabouts of those books are presently unknown. This information may not exist elsewhere. I have attempted to present this information in as simple a format as possible. The soldier's name is followed by his rank, military attachment and age. Unless otherwise indicated the date is the day the burial permit was issued and is followed by the cause and place of death. Section "M" was known as "the soldiers lot."

I am grateful to Robert W. Barnes for the use of his files and for his support and encouragement.

Anna Miller Watring
Dennisport, Massachusetts

MEDICAL FACILITIES IN BALTIMORE 1861-1865

CAMP ANDREW: Established in 1861 on a site which included the confiscated property of Confederate Brigadier General George H. Steuart, Camp Andrew was the home of successive military installations.

CAMP BELGER: Located north of the intersection of Madison and North Avenues, and south of Druid Hill Park, Belger's Barracks were built in 1863.

U.S. GENERAL HOSPITAL, CAMDEN STREET: Conveniently located close to the B. & O. Railroad's Camden Station, this hospital was established early in the war to serve both Union and Confederate soldiers. Set up in buildings occupied by the National Hotel, Camden Street Hospital was in use throughout the war.

JARVIS GENERAL HOSPITAL: Formerly Steuarts Mansion Hospital.

U.S. GENERAL HOSPITAL, McKIMS MANSION: Named Camp McClelland by the 6th. Michigan Regt., this hospital was located south of Greenmount Avenue in an area bounded by the present Preston, Valley, Chase and Homewood Streets. By 1862 a 300 bed hospital was installed in the barracks. This site, the former home of the Little Sisters of the Poor, is now a vacant lot and a playground.

NATIONAL HOTEL HOSPITAL: Also Camden Street Hospital.

U.S. GENERAL HOSPITAL, NEWTON UNIVERSITY: Located on the north side of Lexington, at Calvert Street, this hospital occupied the University buildings and those adjacent.

U.S. GENERAL HOSPITAL, PATTERSON PARK: Located on Patterson Park Avenue at the farther end of Pratt and Lombard Streets, the then Hampstead Hill, Patterson Park was established on land given to the city in 1827 by William Patterson. Converted to Camp Patterson Park, the barracks were built in 1862 after the departure of the 7th Maine Volunteer Regt. In 1863, after temporary occupation by the 9th. Pennsylvania Volunteers, the barracks were converted to a hospital.

STEUARTS MANSION HOSPITAL: Built on the confiscated property of Confederate Brigadier General George H. Steuart, located in an area bounded on the north by W. Fayette and Fairmount (then Montrose) Avenues; on the east by Fulton Avenue; on the south by W. Baltimore Street and on the west by Smallwood Street. Also known as Stuarts Grove and Stuarts Place it was renamed Jarvis General Hospital in 1863. By 1864 its capacity had doubled to 1,500 beds. Bon Secour Hospital now occupies a large part of this site.

U.S. GENERAL HOSPITAL, WEST'S BUILDINGS: Located at Union Dock at the foot of the Jones Falls, south and east of the present Market Place. Convenient for use as a hospital and distribution center for Union and Confederate soldiers.

LOUDON PARK CEMETERY
CIVIL WAR BURIALS

ABBOTT, JAMES H. Co. G, 11th Maine. 19 y/o. 15 Sept. 1862, chronic diarrhea, Lexington St. Hospital. M-337

ABELL, BARTON 71st N.Y. 18 y/o. 26 Sept. 1864, dysentery, Newton. M-1030.

ABOTT, GEO. H. 1st. N.Y. Art. 9 July 1862, typhoid. M-200

ACTON, LOT Co. E, 149th. Ohio. 40 y/o. 15 Aug. 1864, intermittent fever, Camden St. M-923

ACTON. T.L. Co. C, 27th. Ind. 27 y/o. 30 Dec. 1861, typhoid, National Hotel Hospital. M-27

ADAMS, BLAKE B. Confederate prisoner. 20 y/o. 20 May 1862, vault.

ADAMS, ELIJAH Co. B, 52nd. Pa. 19 y/o. 18 Dec.(d. 13 Dec.)1862, diarrhea, West's Buildings. M-490

ADAMS, SABIN G. Co. C, 7th. R.I. 20 y/o. 20 July 1863, diarrhea, West's. M-550

ADDISON, GROVER Co. A, 4th. Vt. 23 y/o. 2 Oct. 1862, typhoid. M-369

ALDRIDGE, JOHN G. Co. H, 5th. Ind. Cavl. 27 y/o. 2 June 1864, starvation. M-806

ALEXANDER, DAVID Pvt. Co. B, 3rd. Md. Regt. 1 Mar. 1862, rubeola, Camden St. Hospital. M-63

ALLEE, EDW. Co. B, 27th. N.Y. 31 July 1862. M-260

ALLEN, ASA C. Co. E, 7th. Maine Regt. 35 y/o. 2 Dec. 1861, consumption, Adams House Hospital. M-11, Body #1

ALLEN, G.A. Co. G, 22nd. Va. C.S.A. 18 Oct. 1864. V-?

ALLEN, JOSEPH Co. ?G/Y, 49th. N.Y. 5 June 1862, Patterson Park. M-157

ALLISON, CORNELIUS Co. D, 124th. N.Y. 13 Dec. 1862, phthisis, Patterson Park. M-476

ALVAH, LOOKER Co. G, 10th. N.Y. 21 y/o. 23 Oct. 1864, typhoid, Jarvis. M-1079

AMES, WILLARD O. Co. F, 17th. Maine. 20 y/o. 24 July 1863, gunshot, Jarvis. M-642

AMIEA, AUGUST Co. G, 10th. N.Y. Art. 5 Aug. 1862. M-280

AMMON, ISAAC Co. M, 100th. Pa. 15 Oct. 186?, dysentery, West's Buildings. M-385

?AMMONT, ALDEN Co. C, 55th. Ohio. 22 y/o. 19 July 1862, typhoid. M-228

AMOND, H.J. Co. B, 83rd. Pa. 10 July 1862. M-203

AMPUTATED LIMBS From hospital. 8 July 1862. M-196

AMYX, JAMES Co G, 10th. Tenn. Cavl. 21 Apr. 1864, diarrhea, West's. M-816

ANDERSON, JAMES Co. C, 11th. Maine. 19 y/o. 3 June 1862, typhoid fever, National Hotel Hospital. M-150

ANDREWS, JAMES F. Co. H, 6th. Mich. 43 y/o. 7 Sept. 1864, ?spine, Jarvis. M-973

ANDREWS, OLIVER G. Co. G, 12th. Conn. 23 y/o. 28 Sept. 1864, gunshot, National. M-1040

APPLING, WM. Confederate soldier. 19th. Ark. Apr. 1863. V-39

ARCHER, GEORGE T. Co. F, 2nd. N.Y. Calv. 32 y/o. 22 Aug. 1864, typhoid, Camden St. M-954

ARMSTEAD, BENJAMIN Co. D, 151st. Pa. Vol. 6 Sept. 186_, McKim's. M-731

ARMSTRONG, HIRAM Co. D, 8th. N.Y. Artl. 24 Apr. 1863, Ft. Masters. Sent home.

ARMSTRONG, JACOB Co. D, 8th. N.Y. 35 y/o. 1 May 1864, ?acute rheumatism, Fed. Hill. Sent home.

ASBURY, GEO. W. Co. G, 40th. Ky. Vol. 15 y/o. 10 May 1864, diarrhea. M-828

ASHBAR, DAVID Confederate soldier. Co. H, 24th. Miss. 24 Apr. 1863, typhoid, " d. at Camden St.". V-39

ASHLEY, RUSSELL D. Co. I, 91st. N.Y. 18 y/o. 16 Oct. 1864, brain, Ft. Marshall. M-1065

ATHON, ALFRED D. Co. C, 21st. Ind. Regt. Capt. Rose. 27 y/o. 5 Feb. 1862, bronchitis. M-50

ATKAINS, WM. Co. F, 8th. Va. 12 Aug. 1962. M-29

ATKINSON, ELIJAH Confederate. Co. C, 5th. N.C. 28 May 1862, "wounded in action at Williamsburg", National Hotel Hospital. Vault

AUSTIN, CHARLES Co. D, 1st. N.Y. 16 Aug. 1864, typhoid fever,Camden St. M-940

AUSTIN, M.G. Co. B, 21st. Va. C.S.A. 24 y/o. 3 Dec. 1863, gunshot wound. V-37

AUSTIN, R.S. 2nd. Lt. 5th N.H. 5 Aug. 1863, gunshot, Prot. Infirmary. M-682

AVERY, LAYMAN Co. I, 9th. N.Y. Cavl. 33 y/o. 15 Aug. 1863, typhoid, Jarvis. M-699

AVERY, ROBERT Co. F, 5th. Mich. 20 y/o. 8 Aug. 1863, brain, Jarvis. M-621

BABCOCK, WM. Co. G, 5th. N.Y. 2 Feb. 1863, typhoid, Patterson Park. M-558

BACON, OSCAR E. Co. E, 8th. Ohio. 20 y/o. 11 Apr. 1864, brain, Camden St. M-767

BAILEY, CALVIN S. Co. F, 3rd. Maine. 36 y/o. 25 Sept. 1864, diarrhea. M-1041

BAILEY, ISAAC Co. E, 11th. Maine. 24 May 1862. M-120

BAILEY, NATHANIEL Co. H, 4th. Vt. 23 y/o. 27 May 1864, erysipelas, Newton. M-864. Sent home.

BAKER, JOHN G. 49th. N.Y. 17 Oct. 1862, typhoid, West's Buildings. M-390

BAKER, NATHAN F. Co. P, 6th. Vermont. 21 y/o. 2 Aug. 1862, typhoid, Newton Univ. M-308

BAKER, WM. F. Co. D, 1st. N.Y. Battery. 17 Aug. 1863, gunshot, McKim's. M-705

BALDWIN, GEO. W. Co. I, 14th. Conn. 30 y/o. 15 Aug. 1863, Jarvis. M-702

BALE_ _?, GILBERT E. Co. G, 15th. Mass. Regt. 20 y/o. 17 Dec. 1862, disease of the heart, Continental. M-491

BALL, JNO. Co. I, 52nd. Pa. 30 May 1862. M-137

BALLENGEE, ANDREW C. Co. D, 8th. Va. 27 y/o. 6 Oct. 1864, diarrhea, Jarvis. M-?1059

BANDO/BADDO, DANIEL Co. C, 93rd. Pa. 13 June 1862, typhoid, Patterson Park General Hospital. M-162

?B/VANNAKER, R. Co. H, 104th. N.Y. 40 y/o. 27 Jan. 1863, typhoid, West's. M-546

BARBER, ALBERT H. 97th, N.Y. 24 Apr. 1864, typhoid fever, Camden St. M-762

BARKER, ALEX Co. F, 22 Mass. 32 y/o. 13 July 1862, typhoid, National Hotel. M-216

BARKER, W.H. Co. E, 13th. Pa. Cavl. 30 y/o. 15 July 1862, hepatitis, McKim's. M-222

BARNES, HY. B. Co. C, 12th. Conn. 35 y/o. 22 Aug. 1864, killed, Camden St. M-955

BARNHAM, JOHN 13 July 1863, gunshot, McKim's. M-613

BARNHARD, MARTIN Co. C, 7th. Mich. Cavl. 20 Apr. 1864, variolosis, West's. M-803

BARNUM, HENRY C. Co. H, 143rd. Pa. Vol. 19 July 1863, gunshot, Camden St. M-695

BARRY, CHARLES Sgt, Co. B, 5th. N.Y. Artl. 7 Oct. 1862. M-374 BART, SEBASTIN Co. H, 6th. N.Y. 17 y/o. 1 Sept. 1864, gunshot wound, Camden St. M-980

BARTHOLOMEW, RANSOM A. Co. H, 114th. N.Y. Vol. 19 Mar. 1863. diarrhea, "died on the Ft. M (?McHenry) Steamer", Nat. Hotel. M-566

BASELEY, W.F. Co. E, 5th. N.Y. 22 y/o. 23 Oct. 1862, typhoid fever, Stewarts. M-411

BASH, JONATHAN Co. E, 1st. Ky. Cavl. 18 Apr. 1864, West's M-815

BASH, WM. Co. G, R. Cavl. 19 Apr. 1864, West's. "died on the boat". M-813

BASSETT, HENRY Co. G, 2nd. Mass. Cavl. 20 y/o. 4 Aug. 1864, typhoid. M-916

BATCHILOR, A. 11 July 1863, McKims. M-610

BATEMAN, (Reads "Robt. Bateman's child") Co. K, 8th. N.Y. 6 Apr. 1863. M-653

BATES, BURDETT Co. G, 2nd. Regt. Pa. Vol. Cavl. 36 y/o. 31 May 1862, phthisis pulmonalis, McKim's Mansion. M-139

BATES, CHARLES E. Co. G, 39th. Mass. 26 Oct. 1864, Jarvis. Sent home.

BATES, OLIVER R. Co. ?I, 76th. N.Y. 22 Jan. 1863. M-551

BAYLEY, JAS. C. Co. F, 5th. Wisc. 28 y/o. 17 Dec.(d. 12 Dec.)1862, dysentery, Nat. Hospital. M-489

BEACH,ERASTUS D. Co. H, 143 N.Y. 20 Mar. 1863, diarrhea, Union Relief. M-560

BEAILS, FRANK Co. G, 101st. N.Y. 31 Oct. 1862. M-4?1

BEALE, MRS. 49 y/o. Nurse at Adam's House. "Next to Brown's". On or after 10 Jan. 1862. M-42

BEAM, MERRIT Co. G, 71st. Penn. Vol. (or N.Y.?). 24 Mar. 1862, pneumonia, Camden St. Hospital. M-73

BECKER, CHARLES Co. A, 82nd. N.Y. 28 y/o. 3 July 1864, typhoid fever, Patterson Park. M-912

BECKWITH, ASPER W. Co. G, 150 Pa. 22 Jul. 1863, vulnis scro., Patterson Park. M-661

?BEEFORD/BECFORD, JOHN F. Co. F, 20th. Maine. 5 Nov. 1862, "died on the cars", National. M-425

BEHLING, CARL Co. E, 26th. Wis. 9 Aug. 1863, gunshot, Jarvis. M-676

BEHRENS, CARL Co. H, 4th. Md. Cavl. 31 y/o. 3 Aug. 1863, typhoid, Camden St. M-667

BELLINGTON, W.T. Co. I, 42nd. Va. C.S.A. 16 Oct. 1864. Vault.

BELLVILLE, THOMAS Co. F, 122nd. Ohio. 37 y/o. 20 July 1864, inflammation of spine. M-895

BEMIS, _ _ Pvt. Co. K, 46th. Mass. 14 July 1863, Ft. Masters. M-696, sent home.

BEMIS, OSCAR Co. E, 34th. Mass. 27 Aug. 1862. M-318

?BENG/BERRY/BING, JAMES Co. G, 50th. N.Y. 36 y/o. 28 Oct. or 8 Nov. (illeg.), 1862, phthisis, Nat. Hotel Hospital. M-420

BENHAM, WM. F. Cpl. Co. C, 21st. Ind. Regt. 28 y/o. 14 Dec. 1861, congestion of _ _ ?. M-36

BENNETT, A.J. Co. E, 12th. R. Island. 30 Mar. 1863, phthisis, West's. M-448

BENNETT, ALBERT M. Co. B, 8th. Mich. 20 y/o. 28 Mar. 1863, pneumonia, West's. M-582

BENNETT, ELIAS Co. F, 122nd. N.Y. Vol. 49 y/o. 24 Aug. 1864, old age, Patterson. M-961

BENNETT, LEONARD Co. G, 118th. N.Y. 2 y/o. 25 Oct. 1864, typhoid, Camp Bradford. M-1082, sent home.

BENTLEY, LEVI Co. E, 14th. N.Y. 26 June 1864, typhoid fever, Jarvis. M-890

BERDGER, ISAAC Co. E, 8th. Mich. 1 Apr. 1864, Pulmonalis, Camden St. M-784

BERENNOYER, E. 20 y/o. Co. D, 8th. N.Y. Artl. 19 June 1864, tetanus, Patterson Park. M-883

BERGMANN, CHR_AS_TON Co. G, 73rd. Pa. Regt. National Hotel. M-21

BERRIAN, JOHN Co. F, 87th. N.Y. 28 y/o. 4 Nov. 1862, Newton. M-317

BERRY, GEO. Co. D, 4th. Tenn. 16 y/o. 26 Dec.(d. 24 Dec.)1862, neuralgia, West's. M-512

BERRYMAN, JOHN Co. A, 3rd. Pa. Artl. 40 y/o. 12 Feb. 1864, "killed by a fall", Camden St. Sent home.

BEVAN, STEPHEN N.C. C.S.A. ca.1862, typhoid. M-42,43

BIDDEL, SAML. H. Co. C, 2nd. Del. 15 July 1863, gunshot, Newton. M-623

BIDDICKS, SAML. Co. H, 5th. Tenn. 16 y/o. 9 Dec. 1862, phthisis, West Buildings. M-465

BIDDLE, J.W. Co. E, 2nd Md. Vol. 19 y/o. 14 Nov. 1863, typhoid fever. M-702

BINKERD, JOHN Co. H, ?4th. Pa. Cavl. 19 y/o. 25 Aug. 1864, typhoid, Patterson. M-9?43

BISB/LY, WILLIAM Co. C, 100th. N.Y. 4 June 1862, typhoid fever, Patterson Park. M-152

BISHOP, DAVID Co. F, 149th. Ohio. 17 June 1864, pneumonia, McKim's.M-874

BISHOPP, HIRAM W. 137th. N.Y. Hospital Steward. 29 Nov. 1862, typhoid. M-448

BLACK, JAMES 25 May 1862, typhoid, National Hotel Hospital. M-121

BLACK, JOHN Co. F, 99th. Pa. 38 y/o. 13 Dec. 1862, diarrhea, National. M-480

BLACK, ROBERT Paymaster. ?—Valley City. 11 Aug. 1862, "died suddenly on bank". M-246

BLACKMORE, J.B. Co. C, 60th. Ohio. 30 y/o. 28 July 1862, typhoid, National Hotel. M-258

BOARTS, GEORGE Co. K, 103rd. Penna. Vol. 12 June 1862, typhoid, Genl. Hospital, Patterson Park. M-163

BODWELL, CHESTER Co. C, 129th. N.Y. 4 Nov. 1862. M-422

BOLAND, MICHAEL Co. E, 17th. Conn. Vol. 5 Sept. 1862, "maria (?mania) portu" ("died on cars"). M-321

BOND, STEPHEN Co. K, 4th. Mich. 54 y/o. 3 July 1864, erysipelas, Camden St. M-933

BONNETT, WM. Co. C, 129th. N.Y. 7 Nov.16. M-428

BORGIAS, CHAS. 20TH. R.I. 74 y/o. 12 Aug. 1864, hemiplegia, Jarvis. M-926

BORT, GEO. D. Co. E, 3?. Mass. 29 y/o. 4 Sept. 1863, typhoid, Newton.

BOSLEY, JAMES Co. D, 2nd. Md. Regt. 25 Jan. 1862, pneumonia, U.S. Genl. Hospital. M-43

BOWEN, JOHN Co. F, 1st. U.S.S.S. 44 y/o. 16 June 1864, gunshot, Camden St. M-910

BOWEN, JOHN Co. D, 12 th. Pa. Cavl. 28 y/o. 16 Sept. 1864, gunshot wound, National. M-1014

BOWER, GEORGE Corp. Co. D, 22nd. Pa. Cavl. 19 y/o. 6 Aug. 1864. M-928

BOYD, J.A. Co. D, 13th. S.C. C.S.A. 20 July 1863, gunshot wound. V-40

BOYER, HENRY Co. D, 93rd. Pa. Vol. 22 y/o. 12 Sept. 1864, gunshot, Camden St. M-996

BRADLEY, PAT 17th. Ind. Battery. 35 y/o. 11 Dec. 1862, typhoid, Stewarts. M-474

BRADSHAW, D.J. Co. B, 51 N.C. C.S.A. 27 Oct. 1864, West's. V-?

BRADY, HUGH Co. T, 104th. Penn. 6 Aug. 1862. M-281

BRANDT, WM. Capt. Co. K, 103rd. N.Y. 35 y/o. 12 Jan. 1863, gunshot, Nat. M-543

BRATZ, AUGUST Co. B, 26th. Wis. 20 y/o. 10 Aug. 1863, gunshot, West's. M-681

BRECKENRIDGE, J.H. Co. F, 148th. Ohio. 26 y/o. 11 Sept. 1864, diarrhea, West's. M-993

BREINIG, JOHN Co. G, 4th. Ky. 43 y/o. 13 May 1864, diarrhea, West's. M-844

BRELL, FRANCIS Co. K, 5th. N.Y. 3 May 1864, jaundice. M-839

BRENNAN, THOS. Co. A, 65th. N.Y. 30 y/o. 25 Oct. 1864, gunshot wound, Jarvis. M-1084

BRENON, MICHAEL 9th. Mass. Vols. 35 y/o. 6 July 1863, compound fracture of skull, Jarvis Genl. Hospital. M-605

BRIANT, JOHN Co. ?I, 5th. N.Y. 18 Dec. 1862. M-488

BRIDGES, JAMES E. Co. C, 156th. N.Y. 20 y/o. 19 Oct. 1864, gunshot, National. M-1097

BRIGHTON, SYLVESTER Co. K, 111th. N.Y. 39 y/o. 26 May 1864, gunshot. M-870

BRINK, NATHANIEL Co. A, 121st. Pa. 19 y/o. 20 Mar. 1864, pneumonia, Camden St. M-776

BRITNER, GEO. Co. I, 8th. Pa. Cavl. 28 y/o. 20 July 1862. M-231

BROADWATERS, NOBLE Co. A, 3rd. Ind. Inf. 16 Aug. 1864, old age, Camden St. M-922

BROGAMIER, JOSHUA Co. I, 7th. Md. 23 y/o. 16 July 1863, diarrhea, National. M-653

BROKAS, JOSEPH Co. D, 98th. Penna. 24 Sept. 1862, "died on steamer Commodore". M-354

BROOKE, GEO. Co. C, 9th. N. York. 17 y/o. 24 Aug. 1864, diarrhea, Patterson. M-952

BROWDIE, JOHN Sgt. Co. H, 82nd. N.Y. 32 y/o. 7 Aug. 1863, gunshot, Newton. M-675

BROWN, CHRISTOPHER Co. E, 58th. Penn. Regt. 23 y/o. 23 Apr. 1862, typhoid, Adams House Hospital. M-84

BROWN, DEXTER Co. H, 15th. N.Y. 24 y/o. 23 Dec.(d. 16 Dec.)1862, dysentery. M-503

BROWN, EDWARD "Soldier, orderly in employ of Maj. Belgen at time of his death". 35 y/o. 8 Dec. 1861, heart disease. Section M, soldiers lot.

BROWN, ELI Co. G, 2nd. Tenn. 23 y/o. 17 May 1864, starvation. M-856

BROWN, ISAAC Conscript. Co. E, 172nd. Pa. 21 y/o. 26 July 1863, typhoid, Newton's. M-691

BROWN, JOHN C. Co. D, 110th. Ohio. 22 y/o. 19 Oct. 1864, diarrhea, Jarvis. M-1099

BROWN, JOHN J. Co. D, 159th. N.Y. 23 y/o. 28 Oct. 1864, gunshot wound, Jarvis. M-1095

BROWN, PHILLIP 39th. N. York. 40 y/o. 13 June 1864, gunshot, Patterson. M-795

BROWN, THOMAS Co. F, 129th. N.Y. 20 Nov. 1862. M-442

BRYANT, GEORGE W. Confederate soldier. Disinterred and remains removed to Philadelphia, Pa. 17 Sept. 1915

BRYANT, JOHN A. Co. D, 21st. Indiana. 1 Mar. 1862, phthisis, Camden St. Hosp. M-62

BUCHANAN, A.L. Co. F, 1st. Pa. R. Co. 44 y/o. 13 Sept. 1862, "wounded in battle at Mechanicsville". M-335

BUCHANAN, WM. H. Co. C, 112th. Ill. 20 y/o. 21 May 1864, debility. M-853

BUCK, WALTER Co. H, 14th. N. Hampshire. 29 y/o. 14 Sept. 1864, Patterson. M-1010

BUEHLER, GEORGE Pvt. Co. D, 2nd. Md. 31 Dec. 1861. M-30

BULIS, CHARLES Co. G, 134th. N.Y. Vol. 19 y/o. 13 Oct. 1862, typhoid, National Hospital. M-381

BUMINGER, WM. Co. D, 5th. Wis. 17 Oct. 1862. M-397

BUMP, WM. H. Co. E, 81st. N.Y. 25 Nov. 1862. M-445

BUNKER, AMBROSE Co. G, 11th. Maine. 20 June 1862, typhoid, Patterson Park. M-170

BUNNELL, FRANKLIN M. Co. A, 2nd. Conn. Art. 20 y/o. 26 Oct. 1864, gunshot wound, National. M-1109

BUNSTON, THOMAS 11th. Va. C.S.A. ca.1862, typhoid. VV-42,43

BURCH, GEO. W. Co. H, 24th. New Jersey. 22 y/o. 2 Apr. 1863, ?balmonlus, Newton Hosp. Sent home.

BURKE, JAMES Co. K, 10th. Md. Vol. 13 Jan. 1864, pneumonia, Fed. Hill. M-754

BURKE, JOHN 1st. Conn. Cavl. 22 y/o. 14 Feb. 1864, peritonitis, Jarvis. M-755

BURNS, HENRY R. 17th. Ind. Battery. 13 Oct. 1962, typhoid, Stewart's Mansion. M-382

BURRELL, WM. Co. G, 11th. Maine. 21 y/o. 5 July 1862, typhoid, National Hotel. M-188

BUSH, JOSEPHUS Co. C, 114th. Ohio. 37 y/o. 17 Sept. 1864, remittent fever, Patterson. M-1017

BUSH, OSCAR M. Co. K, 135th. Ohio. 18 y/o. 3 Aug. 1864, typhoid. M-930

BUTHOLF, SIDNEY Co. D, 56th. N.Y. 21 y/o. 1 Feb. 1863, diarrhea, West's. M-564

BUTLER, EDWARD Co. D, 5th. Art. 2 Dec. 1861, typhoid fever, Adams House Hospital. M-11 (Body #2)

BUTLER, JOHN Co. ?F, 157th. N.Y. 28 y/o. ?1 July 1863, gunshot wound, Jarvis Hospital. M-611

BYRNE, JAMES Co. B, 88th. N.Y. 35 y/o. 26 July 1862, vulnus scloph. M-245

BYRNES, EDWARD Co. B, 131st. N.Y. 44 y/o. 16 Sept. 1862, dysentery, National. M-340

CADEN, MICHAEL Co. G, 73rd. N.Y. 30 y/o. 19 Nov. 1862, dropsy, Stewart's. M-439

CADEY, RILEY B. Co. G, 11th. N. Hampshire. 26 y/o. 12 Apr. 1864, pneumonia, Camden St. M-835

CAHILL, WALTER G. Pvt. Co. J, 21st. Ind. 18 y/o. 8 Mar. 1862, gunshot, Camden St. Hospital. M-67

CALDWELL, W.W. Co. C, 37th. N.C. C.S.A. 22 Oct. 1864, diarrhea. V-?

CAMPBELL, EDW. W. Co. E, 4th. Maine. 24 y/o. 6 Sept. 1862, diptheria, Patterson Park. M-323

CAMPBELL, SAMUEL B. Co. G, ?140th. Pa. 21 y/o. 6 Dec. 1862, diarrhea. M-456

?CANNET, BENJAMIN Co. K, 8th. N.C. Cavl. C.S.A. 14 Oct. 1864, "brought dead to the hospital". V-?86

CAREY, GEORGE T. Co. A, 85th. Pa. Vol. 22 May 1862, typhoid, National Hotel Hospital. M-112

CAREY, JOHN Co. B, 150th. N.Y. 19 y/o. 2 Sept. 1863, typhoid, Camden. M-720

CARLEY, H.M. Co. K, 17th. Vt. 18 y/o. 24 June 1864, Jarvis. M-884

CARLEY, JOHN Co. ?T, 121st. N.Y. 19 y/o. 1 June 1863, drowned. M-448

?CARNULL, WM. H. Co. G, 93rd. N.Y. 11 Aug. 1862, typhoid, Patterson. M-296

?CAROMEL, JAMES M. Co. G, 11th. Va. 22 y/o. 10 Sept. 1864, typhoid, Jarvis. M-976

CARPENTER, HENRY Co. I, 11th. N.C. C.S.A. 40 y/o. 31 July 1863, gunshot. V-38

CARPENTER, HORATIO Co. F, 37th. Mass. 11 Sept. 1864, West's. M-995

CARR, ANDREW Co. F, 1st. Conn. Cavl. 16 y/o. 9 Feb. 1864, pneumonia, Jarvis. Sent home.

CARTER, BENJAMIN Co. C, 1st. ?Berdan S.S.. 18 y/o. 7 July 1862, typhoid. M-190

CASE, ELMER C. Co. E, 10th. Co. 18 y/o. 25 Oct. 1862, diarrhea. M-416

CASTILLIO, JOHN Co. B, 8th. N.Y. H. Artl. 19 y/o. 13 July 1864, gunshot. M-893

CASTILLO, CHAS. Co. F, 16th. U.S. Inf. 24 July 1862, gunshot. M-240

CAUSEY, E.B. "Drafted man". Camp Bradford. 7 Feb. 1863. M-577

CAUSNER, THOS. Co. G, 104th. Pa. 24 June 186?, typhoid, Patterson Park. M-175

CAVANAGH, PETER Co. B, 5th. Md. 5 Aug. 1863. M-683

CAVANNAUGH, JAMES Pvt. Co. D, ?69th. N.Y. Capt. Thomas. 21 Dec. 1861, "res. at Camp". M-24

CAZIER, WM. S. Co. E, 10th. N.Y. 24 y/o. 20 Aug. 1864, pneumonia, Camden St. M-945

CHALFANT, GEO. M. 4th. Wisc. Regt. "Steward at the Hospital". 28 y/o. 21 Dec. 1861, cholera morbus, Adams House Hospital. M-37

CHALLIS, DANIEL Co. F, 5th. New Hampshire. 27 May 1862, cancer, National Hospital. M-127

CHAMBERLIN, EDWARD B. Co. D, 137th. N.Y. 22 y/o. 19 Dec. (d. 18 Dec.) 1862, typhoid, National. M-497

CHAMBERS, GEO. H. Co. A, 8th. Mich. 30 y/o. 16 July 1864, diarrhea, Newton. M-902

CHAMBERS, JOHN Pvt. Co. _J, 9th. Regt. N.Y. S.M. 13 Dec. 1861, dry gangrene, National Hotel Hospital. M-17

CHANDLER, DAMA P. Co. F, 16th. Vermont. 23 y/o. 16 July 1863, gun shot, National. M-658

CHAPLIN, W.H. Co. G, 7th. Maine. 20 May 1862. M-109

CHASE FRANKLIN Co. F, 86th. N.Y. 8 Dec. 1862, phthisis. Sent home.

CHASE, WM. B. Co. D, 7th. Md. Vol. 17 y/o. 18 Feb. 1864, pneumonia, Camden St. M-756

CHASSEN, ENOCH Co. A, 49th. N.Y. 21 y/o. 22 Nov. 1862, heart, West's Buildings. M-444

?CHATT, JOHN S. Co. A, 5th. Mass. 30 y/o. 28 Sept. 1864, National. M-1039

CHITWOOD, H.H. Sgt. Co. G, 2nd. Tenn. 27 y/o. 15 July 1864, diarrhea. M-905

CHRISS, GEO. R. Co. H, 110th. N.Y. 27 y/o. 29 Nov. 1862, vulnus scopt. M-447, sent home.

CHRISTOPHER, STEWART Co. G, 16th. Pa. Cavl. 19 y/o. 23 July 1863, gunshot, Camden St. M-630

CHURCH, THOMAS Co. C, 34th. Va. C.S.A. 29 Oct. 1863, diarrhea. V-37

CHURCHILL, HENRY Co. B, 12th. U.S. Infantry. 25 y/o. 6 Dec. 1862, typhoid. M-260

CLARK, JAMES Co. C, Potomac Home Brigade. 26 y/o. 23 Nov. 1861, typhoid & pneumonia. Grave #1, body #9.

CLARK, JOHN E. Co. H, 21st. Ind. Capt. Rose. 20 y/o. 7 Feb. 1862, cholera morbus. M-53

CLARK, OWEN S. Co. A, 7th. N.J. 22 July 1863, gunshot, West's. M-645

CLARK, WHITMIER "Confederate, native of N.C.". 11 June 1862. "wounded in battle of Williamsburg", National Hotel Hospital. V-42

CLARK, W.J. Miss. C.S.A. 7 Feb. 1862/3?, Calvert St. Hospital. V-42, 43

CLAY, CHARLES M. Co. K, 22nd. N.Y. 19 Oct. 1864, diarrhea. M-1074

CLEMENT, A.F. 16th. Regt. Art. 24 y/o. 1 or 7 Mar. 1864, pneumonia, Newton. Sent home.

CLEVELAND, ERASTUS Co. C, 2nd. Conn. Artl. 25 y/o. 23 Aug. 1864, diarrhea, Camden St. M-953

CLIFFORD, M. Co. I, 2nd. N.Y. 23 y/o. 26 July 1863, pyemia, McKim's. M-689

CLINE, JOHN Co. K?, 89th. Ohio. Paroled prisoner. 22 y/o. 23 Apr. 1864, starvation, Jarvis. M-795, sent home.

CLINE, MARTIN Co. B, 93rd. Pa. 19 y/o. 28 Aug. 1864, diarrhea, Patterson. M-986

CLINTON, THOMAS R. Co. D, 136th. N.Y. 25 y/o. 14 Jan. 1863, phthisis. M-542

CLOUGH, CHARLES E. Co. A, 2nd. Vermont Vol. 18 y/o. 9 July 1863, febris typhoid, Newton University. M-607

COCHREN, J.S. Co. D, 5th. Fla. C.S.A. 26 y/o. 29 Nov. 1863, gunshot wound. V-37

COCHRENE, A.J. Confederate prisoner. Co. E, 41st. Ga. On or after 7 Feb. 1863, Calvert St. Hospital. V-39

COGAN, JOHN Co. ?I, 27th. N.J. 25 Mar. 186?, apoplexy, West Hospital. M-475

COGGSWELL, WM. Co. B, P.R.C. 12 Aug. 1862, typhoid, Stewart's. M-299

COLE, AMBROSE Co. I, 4th. Mich. 19 y/o. 3 July 1864, gunshot, Camden St. M-913

COLE, CHAUNCY. M. Co. C, 3rd. Vermont. 16 y/o. 9 June 1862, typhoid fever, Patterson Park. M-160

COLE, DOMINICK Mc. Co. E, 67th. N.Y. 38 y/o. 26 Oct. 1864, gunshot wound, Patterson. M-864

COLEMAN, CHAS. Co. K, 75th. or 95th. Pa. 29 July 1862. M-253

COLEMAN, TIMOTHY Co. K, 71st. Pa. 4 Aug. 1862. M-276

COLLINS, DAVID 7TH. Maine. 3 Aug. 1862. M-269

COLLINS, LEANDER Co. G, 98th. N.Y. 36 y/o. 29 Nov. 1862, dysentery, National. M-452

COLLINS, PATRICK Co. H, 9th. Mass. Oct. 1863, brain, West Buildings. M-738

COLLINS, VALENTINE Co. B, 90th. Pa. 19 y/o. 23 Oct. 1862, inflamation of bowels, Stewarts. M-410

COLLY, LORENZO Co. G, 25th. N.C. C.S.A. 25 Oct. 1864. Sect. V

COLTON, JOHN Co. F, 14th. Indiana. 22 Aug. 1862. M-314

CONKLIN, M. 21 y/o. 2 Sept. 1862, typhoid, Newton University. M-319

CONNELL, NATHANIEL 19 May 1862, "died on the Vanderbilt". M-103

CONNER, WM. 1st. Penn Ind. Battery. 22 Aug. 1864, typhoid, Camden St. M-948

CONNET, RICHARD B. Co. G, 104th. N.Y. 27 y/o. 7 Jan. 1863, lumbago. West. M-536

CONNOLY, JOHN Co. E, 13th. Pa. Cavl. 4 Aug. 1864, accidental gunshot wound. M-929

CONWAY, A.T. Co. I, 19th. Regt. Maine. 29 y/o. 1 Sept. 1863, Jarvis. M-723

COOK, JOHN Co. D, 7th. Maine. 8 Aug. 1862. M-291

COOLEY, JESSE Co. A, 11th. Ky. Cavl. 53 y/o. 5 May 1864, pulmonalis. M-850

COON, JAMES Co. E, 111th. Pa. 19 June 1862, pneumonia, McKim's Mansion. M-171

COON, WM. 18 Oct. 1862, "taken dead to the hospital from Fortress Monroe", West's Buildings. M-394

COONER, JAMES W. Co. E, 5th. Wisc. 22 y/o. 19 Jan. 1863, typhoid. M-545

CORAH, HENRY Co. K, 4 th. N.Y. 22 July 1862, Patterson Park. M-236

?CORBIN/CORBELL, JAMES Pvt. Co. A, 3rd. Md. Regt. 7 Mar. 1862. M-66

CORNEY, JAMES C. Co. C, 5th. N.Y. Artl. 21 Aug. 1862. M-310

COSGROVE, EDWARD Pvt. 35 y/o. 17 Mar. 1862, consumption, Adams House Hospital. M-71

?CORS/COOS, DAVID Co. H, 75th. Pa. 22 July 1863, gunshot, West's. M-662

COWLEY, DANIEL A. Co. D, 12th. R.I. 29 Dec.(d. 26 Dec.), typhoid, Camden St. M-507

COX, GEO. E. Co. K, 7th. Md. 38 y/o. 17 Aug. 1864, epileptic fit, Jarvis. M-941

COX, ISAAC Co. B, 19th. Pa. Vol. 15 Nov. 1862. M-433

COX, JESSE E. Co. C, 11th. Va. 24 y/o. 21 Aug. 1864, diarrhea, Jarvis. M-946

COX, THOMAS Co. A, 21st. Va. 33 y/o. 15 Aug. 1864, gunshot wound. V-36

COYLE, DANIEL Co. T, 7th. U.S. Inf. 7 Sept. 1863, pulmonalis, Camden St. M-726

CRABTREE, J.B. Co. D, 44th. Tenn. CSA 23 Oct. 1864. Sect. V

CRABTREE, THOMAS Co. L, 1st. Md. Cavl. 34 y/o. 18 May 1863, consumption, Camden St. Hotel. M-597

CRAIG, JOHN H. 5th. Alabama. C.S.A. 26 y/o. "d. 27 July 1863, 11:30 p.m.". 30 July 1863, smallpox. V-38

CRAMER, ANDREW Co. C, 1st. N.Y. Artil. 4 Oct. 1862. M-371

CRAMER, SAMUEL Co. E, 45th. Pa. 32 y/o. 7 July 1864, amputation of arm. M-891

?CRANE/CROW, E.W. Co. H, 11th. Mass. 25 y/o. 28 July 1862, fever, National Hotel. M-257

CRANWELL, THOMAS Co. F, 3rd. Ohio Cavl. 19 Apr. 1864, "died on the boat", West. M-768

CRAP_?, JOHN F. 24 y/o. 7 Sept. 1864, Jarvis. M-977

CRAWFORD, DAVID Co. C, 72nd. N.Y. 24 y/o. "Of N.Y. City". 29 May 1862, "wounded at Williamsburg", Nat. Hotel Hosp. M-134

CRAWFORD, J.R. Confederate prisoner. On or after 7 Feb. 1863. V-39

?CRAWFORD, R.J. Pa. Artl. 22 y/o. 7 Oct. 1864, brain, Jarvis. M-1060

CREAMER, JACOB Co. C, 110th. Pa. 20 y/o. 25 Oct. 1862, typhoid. M-417

CREMER, MICHAEL Co. H, 49th. Pa. 36 y/o. 12 Oct. 1864, typhoid, National. M-1069

CRESSMAN, SAML. W. Co. I, 62nd. Pa. 20 y/o. 21 Aug. 1862, gunshot, National. M-312

CROCKER, E.B.M. Co. F, 122 Ohio. 42 y/o. 18 July 1864. M-903

CROUSE, EMANUEL Co. H, 126th. Ohio. 27 y/o. 21 July 1864, typhoid. M-896

CROW, FIELDING Co. G, 12th. Ill. Cavl. 16 July 1863, typhoid, National. M-652

CROWELL, JONATHON Co. ?J, 14th. N. Hampshire. 39 y/o. 8th. Sept. 1864, diarrhea, Patterson. M-991

CRUMMELL, FREDERICK Co. K, 1st. Ma. Vol. 45 y/o. 3 Oct. 1862, phthisis, Patterson Park. M-362

CUMMINGS, PIERCE J. Co. ?J, 20th. Maine. 34 y/o. 7 Jan. 1863, diarrhea, Nat. Hotel. M-532

CUMMINGS, SAMUEL L. Co. C, 5th. N. Jersey. 9 June 1862, Patterson Park. M-1?7

CUMMINGS, W.H.H. Co. E, 5th. Vt. 4 Aug. 1862. M-277

CUNNINGHAM, JOS. H. Co. D, 2nd. ?Md. 23 y/o. 26 Mar. 1863, diarrhea, Nat. Hotel. M-583

CUNNINGHAM, LORENZO Co. E, 11th. Maine. 4 Mar. 1863, diarrhea, "died at Union Relief Nat. Hosp." M-568

CURCH, BENJ. Co. K, 80th. N.Y. 22 July 1863. M-643

CURLEY, HUGH Co. I, 101st. N.Y. 10 Aug. 1862, heart disease. M-283

CURRIE, JOHN Co. ?I, 17th. Mass. Apoplexy, Patterson Park. M-180

CURRY, JOHN Co. D, 93rd. Pa. 23 y/o. 7 Jan. 186?, diarrhea, Nat. M-529

CURTIS, CHAS. H. Co. H, 5th. Mich. Cavl. 18 y/o. 1 Mar. 1864, measles, Camden. M-758

CUTTER, CHAS. Co. I, 34th. Mass. 19 y/o. 31 July 1864, pneumonia. M-899

CUTTER, DAVID Co. A, 7th. Mich. 9 Dec. 1962. M-464

CYPHAR, JAMES Co. C, 5th. N.Y. H. Art. 21 y/o. 2 Aug. 1864, gunshot wound of hip. M-915

DALTON, THOMAS S. Co. I, 5th. U.S. Battery. 15 July 1863, gunshot, West's. M-619

DAMBUSKEY, HENRY Pvt. Balt. U.S. Engineers. 22 y/o. 23 Feb. 1864, suicide, Camden St. M-760

DANCER, NATHAN Co. I, 55th. Ohio. 24 y/o. 16 July 1862, typhoid, National Hotel. M-221

DANDY, DANIEL Sgt. Co. C, Holcomb S.C. Legion. 14 Oct. 1864, "brought to the hospital dead". V-?

DANFORD, BENJAMIN Co. B, 98th. N.Y. 5 June 1862, typhoid, Patterson Park. M-159

DANIELS, J.W. Co. H, 3rd. N.C. C.S.A. 22 y/o. 22 July 1863, typhoid. V-3

DARROW, EDW. Co. E, 145th. Pa. Vol. 18 Dec. 1862 (d. 13 Dec.), apoplexy, McKim's. M-493

DASSON, AUGUSTUS H. Co. G, 35th. Mass. 23 y/o. 15 Oct. 1862, gunshot, Nat. M-38?

DAVENPORT, D. Co. H, 6th. Vermont. 4 Oct. 1862, diarrhea, McKim's. M-368

DAVENPORT, JAS. HENRY Co. G, 27th. Indiana. 21 y/o. 8 Oct. 1862, Stewart's Mansion. M-376

DAVIDSON, M. Co. B, 145th. Pa. 26 y/o. 4 Oct. 1863, dyptheria, Patterson Park. M-735, sent home.

DAVIDSON, WM. W. Co. I, 57th. Pa. 19 June 1862, Pat. Park. M-168

DAVIS, CHARLES Co. B, 5th. N.Y. Art. 24 y/o. 4 Feb. 1864, smallpox Fort Marshall. M-804

DAVIS, CHRISTOPHER C. Co. J, 9th. Va. Infantry. 20 y/o. 13 Sept. 1864, gunshot, Camden St. M-982

DAVIS, HENRY ?C. Co. C, 9th. N.Y. 32 y/o. 7 Aug. 1863, brain, Jarvis. M-635

DAVIS, JAMES Co. I, Purnell's Legion. 28 May 1862, meningitis, Nat. Hotel Hosp. M-130

DAVIS, JOHN Co. K, 8th. ?Md. 1 Sept. 1863, Ft. Masters. M-718

DAVIS, JNO. Co. J, 93rd. Pa. 24 y/o. 30 Aug. 1864, Jarvis. M-968

DAVIS, JNO. Co. D, 11th. Maine. 30 May 1862. M-135

DAVIS, LONZ'Y P. Co. A, 1st. Pa. Rifles. 21 y/o. 8 Sept. 1862. M-324

DAVIS, PHILIP Co. E, 150th N.Y. 27 y/o. 14 Aug. 1863, Camden St. M-697

DAWSON, JOHN Co. F, 8th. Surgeons. 23 y/o. 28 July 1862, typhoid, Camden St. M-252

DAY, MARION Co. A, 111th. Pa. Vol. 17 y/o. 23 Sept. 1862, gunshot, Nat. Hospital. M-349

DEAN, DUDLEY Co. H, 1st. Ala. 66 y/o. 7 June 1863, diarrhea, Camden St. V-39

DEARBORN, GEO. J. Co. H, 16th. Maine. 19 y/o. 1 Mar. 1863, typhoid, Nat. M-120

DECKER, BENJ. Conscript. 29 y/o. 3 Feb. 1864, pneumonia, Camden St. M-711

DECKER, GIDEO Co. C, 11th. N.Y. 36 y/o. 19 Sept. 1864, dysentery, West's. M-1025

DECOSTA, PETER Co. A, 15th. Maine. 34 y/o. 26 Sept. 1864, diarrhea, National. M-1033

DELAMANE, AUGUSTE Co. K, 58th. N.Y. 50 y/o. 22 Jan. 1863, Calvert St. M-522

DELLENGER, CHARLES Co. A, 87th. Pa. Regt. 1 Apr. 1862, cholera morbus, Camden St. Hospital. M-78

DEMAN, JOHN Co. B, 2nd. Md. Cavl. 21 Oct. 1862, enteritis, McKims. M-404

DEMERY, MYRON Co. H, 24th. Mich. 8 Dec. 1862, erysipelas, Newton. Sent home.

DENNIS, MORRIS Co. I, 153rd. Pa. Vol. 43 y/o. 20 July 1863, exhaustion, Jarvis. M-656

DENNIS, SAMUEL Co. E, 22nd. Mass. 37 y/o. 9 May 1864, diarrhea. M-841

DEVILBISS, STEPHEN Co. A, 45th. Pa. 35 y/o. 30 Sept. 1862, gunshot. M-367

DEVINE, BERNARD Co. L, 18th. Pa. Cavl. 31 y/o. 18 Sept. 1864, diarrhea, Jarvis. M-1049

DEVORE, ANDREW Co. E, 85th. Pa. 31 July 1862. M-268

DEYO, AMOS Co. L?, 133rd. N.Y. 35 y/o. 16 Aug. 1864, "d. on the cars", Camden St. M-924

DILLMAN, CHRISTIAN Co. C, 33rd. N.Y. 44 y/o. 6 Oct. 1862, consumption. M-370

DILLON, A.P. Pvt. Co. K, 27th. Ind. 20 y.o. 25 Jan. 1862, measles, Adams House. M-44

DILYERT, HENRY Co. D, 104th. Pa. Vol. 31 May, 1862, typhoid fever, Nat. Hotel Hosp. M-140

DIMOND, WM. 38 y/o. 21 Dec. 1863, pneumonia, Ft. Marshall. M-747

DIRRS?, SAMUEL Co. B, 3rd. Md. 25 Feb. 1862, typhoid, Camden St. M-61

DIXON, ISAAC Co. E, 11th. N.J. 37 y/o. 3 Aug. 1863, gunshot, West's. M-669

DONAGLEM, E.N. Co. G, 1st. Vt. 15 Oct. 1864, National. M-1098

DONAHUE, EDW. Co. D, 23rd. Pa. 20 y/o. 12 Aug. 1862, Nat. M-298.

DORAN, JOHN Co. K, 1st. Va. 42 y/o. 24 Sept. 1864, typhoid, Patterson. M-1018

DORMAN, JOHN B. Co. K, 1st. N.Y. Dragoons. 43 y/o. 6 Sept. 1864, diarrhea, Jarvis. M-1140

DOUGHERTY, ABRAHAM Teamster, U.S. Army. 30 Oct. 1861, typhoid, Adams House Hosp. M-4

DOUGLASS, NATHANIEL Co. D, Purnell's Legion. 6 May 1862. M-95

DOUGLASS, PETER Co. E, 1st. Md. Regt. Col. Kenly. 22 y/o. 13 Mar. 1862, typhoid. M-68

DOUGLASS, THOMAS M. Co. E, 19th. Ohio. 25 y/o. 19 Sept. 1864, Jarvis. M-1019

DOW, PHIL. H. Co. A, 20th. Mass. Regt. Vol. 22 y/o. 14 Nov. 1861, pneumonia, Adams House Hospital. M-7, body #1.

DREW, A. Co. A, 6th. Ohio Cavl. 1 May 1864, "starvation at Richmond". M-849

DRISCOLL, RICHARD Co. C, 1st. Mass. 25 y/o. 15 Aug. 1862, typhoid. M-304

DUBOE, PAUL Co. C, 3rd. Md. Cavl. 26 Oct. 1863, brain, Newton. M-741

DUDLEY, AARON Co. E, 31st. Marines. 31 y/o. 9 Aug. 1864, typhoid. M-918

DUNCAN, ?FRELLBONN Co. B, 21st. Indiana. 25 y/o. 26 Dec. 1861, typhoid fever, Adams House. M-25

DUNN, JAMES B. 1st. Sgt. Co. K, 13th. Conn. 31 y/o. 2 Oct. 1864, Jarvis. M-1052

DUNN, JOHN Co. B, 41st. N.Y. 30 y/o. 5 Aug. 1863, gunshot, Newton. M-672

DUNN, WILLIAM Co. ?G, 4th. Pa. Cav. 17 y/o. 25 Aug. 1864, typhoid, Jarvis. M-962

DUNTON, ?ASA/OSRA C. Co. K, 60th. N.Y. Regt. 30 Jan. 1862. M-48

DUPRO, LOUIS Co. A, 60th N.Y. 2 Jan. 1862. M-32

DURLAND, ALBY Co. F, 5th. N.Y. Artl. 22 y/o. 4 Sept. 1863, typhoid, Camden St. M-721, sent home.

DURPHY, HENRY Co. C, 6th. Vermont. 22 y/o. 18 June 1864, typhoid fever, Patterson. M-935, sent home.

DYER, E. ?J. Co. B, 20th. Maine. 5 Jan. 1862, phthisis, McKims. M-526

DYKEMAN, JOHN 3 Apr. 1864, pneumonia, Ft. Marshall. M-811

EAGEN, WM. Co. E, 17th. N.Y. 23 ?__ 1863. M-576

EARLY, PATRICK Co. F, 170th. N.Y. 49 y/o. 21 Oct. 1862, "killed on the cars", National. M-402

ECKER, TOLINT. Co. A, 22nd. Pa. 23 y/o. 19 Oct. 1864, gunshot wound, Jarvis. M-1096

EDWARD, ARCHIBALD Co. E, 21st. Va. 14 y/o. 6 Aug. 1864, gunshot wound. V-36

EDWARDS, A.R. Co. R, 26th. N.C. CSA 23 y/o. 3 Aug. 1863, amputation of leg. V-33

EGAN, JOHN P. 19 May 1862, "died on the Vanderbilt". M-102

EGAN, LAWRENCE Co. C, 8th. Md. 29 y/o. 7 Feb. 1863, gastritis. M-573

ELDER, CHARLES Co. C, 142nd. Pa. 17 y/o. 30 Dec.(d. 27 Dec.)1862, typhoid, Nat. Hotel. M-518

ELLIS, WM. Co. C, 15th. Mass. 23 y/o. 5 Jan. 1863, diarrhea, Stewart's M-522

ELLISON, BENJAMIN F. Co. A, 15th. Va. Inf. 20 y/o. 2 Oct, 1864, typhoid, National. M-1052

EMERY, J. ATHAN. Co. G, 14th. U.S. Inf. 17 y/o. 20 Sept.1862, typhoid. M-334

ENGLISH, HENRY Co. A, 176th. N.Y. 30 y/o. 19 Oct. 1864. M-1075

ENGLISH, JOHN Co. E, Purnell's Legion. 21 y/o. 25 Oct. 1862. M-413

EPSON, WILLIAM Co. G, 2nd. Tenn. 18 y/o. 23 May 1864, bronchitis. M-868

ERNST, CHARLES Co. B, 40th. N.Y. 18 y/o. 3 Aug. 1863, gunshot, Jarvis. Sent home.

EVANS, MATTHEW Co. K, 22nd. Regt. 2nd. Balt. Corps. 28 y/o. 25 Mar. 1864, diarrhea, Newton. M-782

EVERETTS, J.R. Co. G, 2nd. Tenn Inf. 4 May 1864, "starvation at Richmond". M-840

FAIR, JOSEPH Co. L, 14th. Pa. Cavl. 52 y/o. 5 Aug. 1863, gunshot, Jarvis. M-674

FALDA, HUGO 5th. Md. 25 Nov. 1863, consumption. M-745

FALLS, STEPHEN W. Co. F, 1st. Pa. Rifles. 21 y/o. 28 Apr. 1864, diarrhea, West's. M-822

FARNSWORTH, JEROME Co. G, 1st. Marines. 19 y/o. 27 July 1863, gunshot. M-638

FAUTHOO?S, GEO. W. 60th. Priv. Signal Corps. 30 y/o. 17 Sept. 1864, typhoid fever, West's. M-1006

FENTON, JOHN L. 9th. Mass. Battery. 28 y/o. 3 Aug. 1863, gunshot, Jarvis. M-66, sent home.

FERGUSON, JOHN Co. B, 1st. Ind. 26 Sept. 1862, typhoid. M-355

FIELD, EUGENE Ord. Sgt. 2nd. Md, Rebel Cavl. 34 y/o. 16 July 1864, "gunshot by Ishmail Day". V-36

FINCH, WM. Co. F, 98th. N.Y. 50 y/o. 3 July 1864, gunshot, West's. M-911

FINNEY, MICHAEL 7 Aug. 1863, Camden St. M-625

FISHER, ?F/T. Co. G, 17th. Mich. 22 Mar. 1863, typhoid ("died on his way from Newport News"). M-580

FISHER, THOMAS Co. A, 25th. N.Y. 47 y/o. 16 Sept. 1864, typhoid, Patterson Park. M-1004

FISK, FRANKLIN Co. ?J, 19th. Maine. 17 y/o. 16 July 1863, pneumonia, Jarvis. M-657

FISKE, SQUIRE Co. G, 3rd. Md. P.H.B. 24 y/o. 15 Oct. 1864, typhoid, Jarvis. M-1067

FITCH, ISAAC Co. ?J, 85th. N.Y, 23 y/o. 10 July 1862, diarrhea, National. M-205

FLEMMING, WM. H. Co. E, 74th. N.Y. 20 May 1862. M-107

FLETCHER, RILEY E. Co. A, 50th. N.Y. Vol. 22 May 1862, typhoid, Nat. Hotel Hosp. M-111

FLINT, ELIJAH Co. B, 37th. Mass. 37 y/o. 7 July 1864. M-906

FLOOD, WM. (or JESSE KITCHEN?) Co. C, 77th. N.Y. 24 y/o. 23 July 1862, typhoid fever, National Hotel. M-238

FOGG, T.G. Co. F, 20th. Maine. 23 Feb. 1863, phthisis, Nat. Hotel. M-572

FORD, JAMES H. Recruit. 18 y/o. 4 Jan. 1864, typhoid, Camden St. Sent home.

FORD, JOHN Co. ?I, 1st. Mich. Cavl. 34 y/o. 1 Sept. 1864, gunshot wound, Camden St. M-970

FORLEY, JOHN Co. I, 9th. Md. 20 Apr. 1864, diarrhea, West's. M-816

FOSS, GEO. H. Co. C, 5th. Maine. 28 y/o. 13 July 1862, typhoid. M-217

FOSS, RALPH H. Co. A, 20th. Maine. 15 Dec. 1862, typhoid. M-482

FOSSELMAN, WILLIAM Co. E, 202nd. Pa. 19 y/o. 8 Oct. 1864, typhoid, National. M-1061

FOSTER, A.B. Co. K, 64th. Ga. 19 Oct. 1864. V-?

FOWLE, SETH Co. H, 11th. Maine. 22 y/o. 11 Dec. 1862, chronic diarrhea, West. M-469

FOWLER, WM. Co. D, 91st. Ohio. 21 y/o. 22 Sept. 1864, typhoid fever, Jarvis. M-1046

FOX, ALEX Co. F, 8th. N.Y. 7 Feb. 1863. M-547

FRAY, THOMAS Co. G, 14th. N. York. 22 July 1863, gunshot, West's. M-641

FREDERICK, WILLIAM 3rd. Ga. C.S.A. 23 Dec. 1862, typhoid. V-42,43

FREEAR?, DUBOIS Co. I, 57th. Pa. 3 June 1862. M-151

FRENCH, J.G. CO. E, 57th. N.H. 16 Sept. 1862, dysentery, Patterson Park. M-339

FRICK, J.D. Co. C, 1st. S.C. Rifles. C.S.A. 19 y/o. 1 Sept. 1863, fever. V-37

FRIDLINE, HARRISON Co. J, 163rd. Ohio. 22 y/o. 4 Sept. 1864, typhoid, Camden St. M-971

FRISBY, K. Co. ?J, 10th. Mass. 13 July 186?. M-219

FRITZ, SAMUEL Co. E, 111th. N.Y. 22 y/o. 19 July 1863, gunshot, Jarvis. M-648

FRY, ALBERT F. Co. F, 17th. Mass. Regt. 28 Dec. 1861, Camp Stewart. M-26

FULLER, GEO. A. Co. G, 129th. N.Y. 25 Oct. 1862. M-380

FULLER, SANFORD K. Andrews Sharp Shooters. 19 July 1863, amputation, McKim's. M-634

FULLER, WM. W. Co. C, 83rd. Pa. 25 y/o. 20 Nov. 1862, apoplexy. M-441

FULTON, DAVID Co. G, 111th. N.Y. 25 y/o. 27 July 1863, gunshot, Jarvis. M-690

FULTON, JOHN 49th. Pa. Vol. Col. Irvine. 24 y/o. b. Pa. 23 Sept. 1861, "killed on the R.R.". DD-63

GAGE, WM. H. Co. H, 13th. Mass. 23 y/o. 21 Aug. 1863, "gangreen", Jarvis. M-711

GAINES, ALLEN W. 28 y/o. 2 June 1862, typhoid, Camden St. Hosp. M-145

GALLIGIN, THOMAS Co. K, 188th. Pa. 35 y/o. 16 Sept. 1864, dropsy, West's. M-1003

GALLOWAY, J.I. Co. C, 4th. Md. 29 Jan. 1864, consumption, Patterson Park. M-752

GARDEN, E.B. Co. J, 47th. Ala. Bur. 23 Dec. 1864, Conf. Hill, A-1

GARDNER, ABRAM. Co. K, 128th. N.Y. 46 y/o. 29 Nov. 1862. M-450

GARDNER, DANIEL (DAVID GORDON written on side) Co. E, 12th. New Jersey. 31 y/o. 7 Feb. 1862, brain. M-562

GARDNER, H.W. Co. C, 1st. S.C. Bur. Nov. 1864, Conf. Hill, Row B.

GARDNER, SAML. O. Co. H, 2nd. Md. Regt. 35 y/o. 2 Dec. 1861, "killed by his Officer". M-50

GARLAND, JAME K. Co. A, 2nd. Tenn. 22 y/o. 6 May 1864, diarrhea, West's. M-852

GARNER, WM. T. Teamster. 22 Dec. 1863. M-750

GARRETT, W.B. Co.D, 18th. S.C. Bur. 15 Oct. 1865, Conf. Hill, Row B

GARTMAN, WM. Co. F, 69th. Pa. 18 y/o. 10 Sept. 1862, gunshot, National. M-328

GATES, ALBERT F. Co. C, 7th. Maine Regt. Vol. 22 y/o. 7 Nov. 1861, pneumonia, Adams House Hospital. M-5

?GAWM, CHARLES Pvt. Co. B, 3rd. Vt. 4 Jan. 1862, phthisis, Nat. Hotel Hosp. M-34

GEBO, THEODORE Co. I, 92nd. N.Y. 21 y/o. 21 July 1862, typhoid. M-232

GEER, JOHN Pvt. Co. D, 6th. N.Y. 19 Dec. 1861, typhoid fever, Camp at Mt. Clare. (Notation on opp. pg. "This name, I think, should be HUGH ADDERION".) M-32

GELATT, C.W. Co. A, 56th. Pa. 19 y/o. 23 June 1864, diarrhea, Newton. M-100

GENTREE, E.B. Bur. 23 Dec. 1864, Conf. Hill, A-3.

GEORGE, DANIEL G. Co. K, 8th. Ill. Cavl. 24 y/o. 4 Jan. 1863, bronchitis, Newton University. M-521

GESLER, JACOB Co. D, 8th. Md. 33 y/o. 9 Dec. 1862, typhoid, National. M-463

GIBBINS, _ _ ? Buried 30 Dec. 1863, Conf. Hill, A-?

GIBBS, Benj. 21 y/o. Typhoid fever. 23 Oct. 1864. M-1081

GIBSON, E.T. Co. H, 56th. Va. 27 y/o. Bur. 20 Aug. 1863, Conf. Hill.

GIBSON, H.T. Co. H, 56th. Va. C.S.A. 27 y/o. 20 Aug. 1863, gunshot wound. V-37

GIBSON, R.W. Co. I, 21st. S.C. Bur. 17 Oct. 1864, Conf. Hill, A-?

GIFFORD, GEO. W. Co. D, 11th. Pa. 13 July 1862, typhoid, Nat. M-218

GILDY, GEO. W. Co. E, 78th. N.Y. 23 y/o. 23 July 1862, corditis?. M-239

GILLIGAN, JAMES Co. H, 104th. Penn. 29 y/o. 31st. May 1862, typhoid fever, Nat. Hotel Hosp. M-141

GILLISON, MATTHEW Co. T?, 11th. Pa. R.C. 47 y/o. 27 Sept. 1862, anasarca?, Stewart's Mansion. M-3?

GILPEN, JOHN Co. F, 22nd. Buried 15 Oct. 1864, Conf. Hill, Row C.

GIVANS, GEO. W. 28th. Va. C.S.A. 18 May 1862, gunshot. Vault

GIVANS, GEORGE H. 25th. Va. Bur. 18 May 1862, Conf. Hill, Row C.

GLADFELTER, JACOB G. Battery L, 5th U.S. Artl. 1 Aug. 1862, syphillis, Stewart's. M-271

GLASBY, WM. Teamster. 21 y/o. 10 Aug. 1864, diarrhea, Patterson. M-921

GLASGOW, ROBT. Co. F, 1st. Pa. Artl. 24 y/o. 16 Aug. 1864, typhoid, Jarvis. M-958

GLEASON, WM. Co. M, 8th. N.Y. Cavl. 22 y/o. 3 Feb. 1863, rheumatism, Newton. M-714

GLENNING, THOMAS 4 Nov. 1861, pneumonia, Nat. Hotel Hosp. M-3, body #2

GOBLE, PETER Co. E, 159th. Ohio. 20 y/o. 16 Aug. 1864, typhoid, Jarvis. M-939

GODWIN, DENNIS L. C.S.A. 15 May 1862. Vault

GOHOMET, J.G. 6th. Mich. Artl. 23 Dec.(d. 21 Dec.)1862, diarrhea, National. M-501

GOLD, WALTER Co. E, 103rd. Pa. 5 June 1863, pneumonia, Patterson Park. M-123

GOLVIN, FRANCIS 98th. N.Y. Regt. 29 May 1862, typhoid, Patterson Park. M-131

GOOD, GEO. Co. B, 7th. Va. 18 y/o. 30 Dec.(d. 25 Dec.)1862, dysentery, Nat. Hotel. M-519

GOODNOUGH, HARWOOD Co. G, 98th. N.Y. 23 y/o. 31 Sept. 1864, diarrhea, West's. M-1035

GOODRICH, ALLEN W. Co. C, 11th. Vt. 25 y/o. 19 Sept 1864, gunshot in thigh, Canden St. M-1018

GOODSELL, ANDREW G. Co. H, 8th. Mich. 38 y/o. 3 July 1864, gunshot, Patterson. M-907

GOODWIN, E.W. Co. A, 11th. Miss. Bur. 30 Dec. 1863, Conf. Hill, Sect. A.

GOODWIN, FRANK 8th. Ga. Regt. C.S.A. 19 y/o. 21 July 1863, "killed 2 July at Gettysburg". M-40. Sent home to Savannah, Ga. 1 May 1867.

GOODWIN, FRANK 8th. Ga. 19 y/o. Buried 21 July 1863, Conf. Hill, Row C

GOODWIN, R.W. Co. A, 11th. Miss. C.S.A. 30 Dec. 1863, gunshot wound. M-37

GO(R/S)AN(F/B)LE, JOHN Co. B, 5th. P.H.B. 25 y/o. Diarrhea. Buried 29 Nov. 1862.

GOSLEE, GEO. H. Co. D, 3rd. Del. Vol. 20 y/o. 24 Nov. 1862, diarrhea, Patterson Park. Sent home.

GOUGH, NELSON Co. C, 3rd. N.Y. 31 May 1862, cerebolis?, Camp Federal Hill. M-142

GRAFTEN, JAMES Pvt. 27 Jan. 1862, typhoid, U.S. Hospital, Camden St. M-46

GRAFTON, E.G. Bugler?. 1st. Maine. 20 y/o. 10 Aug. 1862, "killed on the R.R.". M-293

GREEN, ALBERT C. Co. H, 1st. R.I. Cavl. 29 y/o. 1 May 1864, abcess, West's. M-825

GREEN, CHARLES Co. C, 18th. Mass. 20 y/o. 12 July 1862, typhoid, National. M-215

GREEN, DAVID Co. B, 18th. Conn. 44 y/o. 19 June 1863, typhoid fever, Ft. Marshall. M-601

GREEN, ELIJAH 5th. N.Y. Artl. 18 y/o. 13 Mar. 1864, typhoid, Ft. Marshall. M-761

GREEN, JOHN Co. H, 148th. Pa. 16 Aug. 1863, gunshot, McKim's. M-701

GREEN, JOS. W. Co. E, 15th. Pa. Cavl. 26 y/o. 20 Sept. 1864, typhoid fever, Jarvis. M-1021

GREEN, OSACR G. 5th. N.Y. Artl. 18 y/o. 16 Mar. 1864, pneumonia, Camden St. M-771

GREEN, WM. H. Co. A, 7th. R.I. 22 Apr. 1863, pneumonia, West's. Sent home.

GREGG, JOSEPH Musician. 7th. Ind. 23 July 1863, contusion of head, Newton. M-628

GRIFFEY, WM. F. Co. G, 1st. Ct? Cavl. 7 Apr. 1864, Jarvis. M-820

GRIFFIN, JOSEPH L. 10th. N.Y. Cavl. 5 Sept. 1862, typhoid, Patterson Park. M-320

GRIFFITH, EDW'D Co. L, 3rd. Pa. Cavl. 4 Sept. 1862, Stewarts. M-198

GROFF, JACOB Co. K, 96th. Penn. 31 y/o. 18 Apr. 1863, diarrhea, McKims. M-586

GROSS, WENDLIN New York Battery. 20 Apr. 1863. M-593

GROUX, GUSTAVUS Pvt. Co. I, 5th. Md. Regt. 24 Jan. 1862. M-42

GUNDRUM, JOSHUA Co. H, 123rd. Ohio. 19 y/o. 24 Sept. 1863, "gangreen", Jarvis. M-735

GURTHER, ABNER Co. G, 11th. Vt. 29 Aug. 1864, typhoid fever, McKims. M-694

GUTHREY, MARION Co. J, 1st. Ala. Cavl. 21 Apr. 1864, bronchitis, West's. M-764

GWYNN, THOS. W. 87th. Pa. Regt. 38 y/o. 17 Apr. 1862, consumption, Adams House. M-81

HAGADORN, PORTER Co. K, Berden Sharpshooters. 26 May 1862, gunshot, Patterson Park. M-97

HAGGERLY, PATRICK Co. E, 5th. N.C. C.S.A. b. Ireland. 23 May 1862, National Hotel. Vault

HAINES, JOHN W. Pvt. Co. L, J__Harris's Cavl. 23 Nov. 1861, typhoid & pneumonia, Nat. Hotel Hosp. M-8, body #2.

HALE, RATHAN Co. A, 16th. Conn. Vol. 15 Oct. 1862, typhoid.

HALL, JOHN L. 17th. Ind. Bat. 18 y/o. 9 Dec. 1862, typhoid. M-466

HALL, LUCIUS Co. F, 5th. Wisc. 20 y/o. 21 July 1862, typhoid. M-230

HALPIN, WILLIAM Co. A, 5th. N.Y. Art. 10 Sept. 1863, Ft. Masters. M-73

HAMLIN, GILMAN Co. I/J?, 6th. N.Y. 13 Oct. 1862. M-38

HAMMER, JOSEPH D. Co. D, 142nd. Pa. Vol. 24 y/o. 8 Sept. 1863, gunshot wound, Camden St. Hosp. M-730

HAMMOND, EDW. P. Co. K, 1st. Ohio Artl. 19 y/o. 16 Sept. 1962, Stewarts. M-342

HAMMOND, WM. E. Co. E, 1st. Ma. Cavl. 29 Aug. 1863, diarrhea, Union R. Rooms. M-724

HAMMONTREE, JAMES Co. D, 110th. Ohio. 43 y/o. 16 Sept. 1864, diarrhea, Jarvis. M-1007

HANCE, JAMES H. Co. C, 30th. Marines. 17 y/o. 29 Aug. 1864, diarrhea, Patterson. M-981

HANCOCK, H.D. Co. G, 12th. Ala. C.S.A. 16 Oct. 1864. V-?

HANKS, WYATT Confederate soldier. Apr. 1863. V-39

HANN, HENRY Co. K, 68th. N.Y. 27 y/o. 14 Dec. 1863, bronchitis, Camden St. M-743

HAPMAN, R.M. Co. F, 150th. N.Y. 41 y/o. 26 Aug. 1863, Jarvis. M-716

HARD, THOMAS Co. D, 42nd. N.Y. 30 y/o. 22 Nov. 1862, typhoid, Stewarts. M-443

HARDING, GEO. Co. C, 5th. Art. 23 Oct. 1862. M-406

HARDMAN, H. Co. D, 10th. Va. 20 y/o. 14 Sept. 1864, gunshot, Jarvis. M-999

HARDY, HENRY Co. K, 4th. Wisc. 24 y/o. 14 Mar. 1862, typhoid, Camden St. Hosp. M-70

HARLBUT, JESPER Co. I, 120th. N.Y. 22 y/o. 15 Aug. 1863, gunshot, West's. M-703

HARMAND, AUGUST Co. C, 98th. Pa. 50 y/o. 28 July 1862, diarrhea, National Hotel. M-251

HARNISH, ALLEN Co. EE, 5th. Pa. R.C. 21 y/o. 22 July 1862, sclop., Camden St. M-235

HARRINGTON, O. Co. G, 49th. N.Y. 14 June 1862, typhoid, McKims Mansion. M-124

HARRIS, BRADFORD D?. 8 Sept. 1864, typhoid, Camden St. Sent home.

HARRIS, JOHN T. Co. H, 4th. Vermont. 20 Sept. 1862, phthisis. M-347

HARRIS, JOSEPH Co. E, 49th. Pa. Vol. 24 y/o. 30 June 1864, gunshot, Camden St. M-889

HARRIS, WM. C. Co. I, 16th. Ill. Cavl. 23 Apr. 1864, diarrhea, West's. M-766

HARRISON, GEO. Co. I, 10th. Va. 23 y/o. 16 Aug. 1864, diarrhea, Camden St. M-959

HARRYMAN, E.R. Co. E, Purnell's Legion. 15 June 1862, McKim's Mansion. M-109

HARTWELL, WILLIS Co. H, 2nd. Conn. 42 y/o. 29 Oct. 1864, typhoid, Newton. M-1093.

HATHAWAY, AUGUSTIN Co. D, 7th. Pa. R.C. 24 y/o. 15 Aug. 1862, typhoid. M-302,

HATHAWAY, JOHN Co. K, 61st. N. York. 43 y/o. 23 June 1864, diarrhea, Newton. M-886

HATHAWAY, SETH H. Co. B, 23rd. Wis. 41 y/o. 7 Jan. 1863, diarrhea, Nat. Hotel. M-534

HAUBER, JOHN Co. C, 2nd. Md. 47 y/o. 25 Oct. 1862, gunshot. M-377

HAUFET, HARRY Co. D, 20th. N.Y. 1 June 1863, National Hotel. M-447

HAUGHAVUK?, LEFFORD Co. D, 3rd. N.J. 40 y/o. 9 June 1864, gunshot, Camden St. M-774

HAUPTMAN, CHSRLES Co. B, 159th. Ohio. 40 y/o. 7 Aug. 1864, cholesteremia, Patterson Park. M-930

HAVEN, W.W. Co. I, 4th. Mich. 24 y/o. 25 July 1862, gunshot. M-241

HAVENS, CHAS. 2nd. Pa. Cavl. Measles, Camden St. M-819

HAWKINS, HENRY Co. B, 72nd. Pa. 23 y/o. 20 July 1863, schopetimus?, Newton. M-647

HAYES, EDWARD Co. C, 2nd. N.Y. 24 Apr. 1864, typhoid, West's. M-793

HAYES, JAMES Co. B, 7th. Mass. 9 June 1862, pneumonia, Patterson Park. M-161

HAYS, D.W. Co. H, 1st. Me. H.Artl. 19 June 1864, typhoid fever, West's. M-985

HAYS, HOWARD R. Sgt. Co. C, 21st. Ind. 32 y/o. 13 Dec. 1861, typhoid. M-38

HEALD, W.H. Co. F, 2nd. Mass. Vol. 14 Dec. 1861, typhoid. M-19

HEALY, JOHN Co. A, 140th. N.Y. 25 y/o. 25 Aug. 1863, gunshot, Jarvis. M-717

HEFFNER, C.R. Co. F, 38th. N.C. 14 Oct. 1864, "brought dead to the hospital". V-_?

HELLEN, HANK "Soldier". Co. C, 100th. N.Y. 26 July 1862, phthisis pulmonalis. M-247

HENDERBACK, GUSTAVIS Co. J, 17th. N. York. 28 y/o. 20 Mar. 1863?, diarrhea. M-559

HENDERSON, OLIVER P. Co. E, 85th. Pa. Vol. 26 May 1862, typhoid, Camden St. M-123

HENDERSON, SAMUEL Co. G, 83rd. Pa. 6 Aug. 1862. M-285

HENDERSON, THOMAS Co. D, 1st. Mich. 16 y/o. 15 Mar. 1864, pneumonia, Camden St. M-770,

HENMEGER, DAVID Co. C, 8th. Pa. 27 May 1862, typhoid, National Hotel Hosp. M-128

HENRY, ANDREW Co. I, 142nd. N.Y. 31 y/o. 10 Oct. 1864, gunshot, West's. M-979

HENRY, JACOB Co. E, 5th. Ma. 21 June 1863. M-598

HENRY, WM. 103rd. Pa. Vol. 10 July 1862. M-208

HEROY?, WM. Co. E, 120th. N.Y. 19 Apr. 1864, "died on the boat, with starvation". M-834

HERZBERGER, BALTHIYAN? Co. A, 58th. N.Y. 43 y/o. 11 Dec. 1862, diarrhea, Stewart's. M-470

HESTON, SAMUEL Co. B, 45th. Ohio Vol. Paroled prisoner. 22 Apr. 1864, diarrhea, West's. M-791

HEWES, WILLIAM Co. E, 27th. Mo. 30 y/o. 10 May 1864, starvation. M-847

HEWITT, H.W. Pvt. Co. J, 111 Pa. Vol. 30 Apr. 1862, measles. M-91

HEWITT, SAML. G. Pvt. Co. F, 17th. Regt. Mass. Vol. 19 y/o. 23 Apr. 1862, pneumonia, Adams House Hosp. M-85

HICKEY, JOHN Co. C, 28th, Mass. 19 y/o. 17 Aug. 1863, Newton. M-704

HICKS, BENJAMIN F. Co. L, 1st. Mich. 25 y/o. 21 Oct. 1864, dysentery, Patterson. M-930

HIGGENS, MARTIN E. Co. E, 73rd. N.Y. 26 y/o. 16 July 1863, vulnus sclop., Newton. M-654

HIGGINS, H. Corp. Co. G, 11th, Maine. 23 Sept. 1862. M-351

HINES, JOSEPH 21 May 1862, National Hotel Hosp. M-118

HINTON, JAMES Co. A, 111th. Pa. Vol. 1 May 1862. M-113

HODSON, CYRUS Co. G, 149th. Ohio. 39 y/o. 8 June 1864, brain, Ft. Marshall. Sent home.

HOFFER, JOHN Co. B, 48th. N.Y. 23 y/o. 1 May 1864, diarrhea. M-?

HOFFMAN, WILLIAM Co. C, 131st. N.Y. 32 y/o. 29 Sept. 1864, gunshot, National. M-1072

HOGUE, HARRISON Co. I/J?, 105th. Pa. 23 y/o. 12 Dec. 1862, pulmonalis, Continental _ _. M-472

HOLDER, THOMAS S. Co. B, 1st. Ky. Cavl. 25 y/o. 4 May 1864, debility, West's. M-851

HOLENBECH, NELSON Co. F, 7th. N.Y.H.A. 37 y/o. 26? Aug, 1864, gunshot wound of left leg, Patterson. M-9454

HOLLERTON, NELSON Co. K, 4th. Pa. 29 July 1862. M-260

HOLMAN, JAMES Co. G, 15th. Va. 21 y/o. 26 Oct. 1864, pneumonia, Jarvis. M-1112

HOLME, M.H. Co. C, 1st. N.C. Cavl. C.S.A. 21 Oct. 1864. Sect. V

HOLMES, ALEX C. Co. B, 77th. N.Y. 31 y/o. 23 Oct. 1862, typhoid. M-409

HOLMES, JAMES Co. A, 1st. U.S. Inf. 31 y/o. 15 Sept. 1864, diarrhea, West's. M-1011

HOLSMAN, G. Co. L, 5th. U.S. Art. 3 Sept. 1962, Stewart's. M-196

HOLT, _ _? 11 Nov. 1862, "killed on the rail road". Sent home.

HOMDORFF, JOHN Co. D, 1st. Md. Cavl. Regt. 4 Feb. 1862. M-49

HOMER, ELIJAH A. Co. B, 72nd. N.Y. 17 y/o. 23 July 1963, gunshot, Jarvis. M-625

HONE, HARRISON 22nd. Maine Cavl. 21 y/o. 20 Nov.(d. 31 Oct.)1862, typhoid. M-431, sent home.

HOOK, JOHN Co. H, 49th. Pa. 28 y/o. 24 May 1864, gunshot. M-869

HOPKINS, SHERMAN Co. L?, 6th. Mich. 30 y/o. 15 Sept. 1864, typhoid fever, Patterson Park. M-1012

HORNER, _ _? 6th. Vt. 28 July 1862, typhoid, National. M-255

HORTEN, PETER Co. H, 3rd. Md. Vol. 31 July 1862, diarrhea, Patterson Park. M-267

HORTON, CHARLES Co. H, 26th. Mich. 21 y/o. 5 Mar. 1864, Camden St. M-774

HOVEY, OLIVER Co. D, 81st. N.Y. 19 y/o. 2 Oct. 1862, gunshot, Nat. Hotel Hosp. M-366

HOWARD, H.H. 1st. Maine. 10 July 1863, "gangreen", McKims. M-608 HOWARD, IRA F. 23 y/o. 10 apr. 1863, bronchitis, Camden St. M-587

HOWARD, JAMES Pvt. Co. A, 2nd. Md. Regt. Capt. Haney. 28 y/o. 14 Dec. 1861, Mt. Clare. M-18

HOWE, DANIEL Co. L, 5th. U.S. Artl. 28 y/o. 24 Jan. 1863, Stewart's. M-549

HOWELL, WM. Co. L, 27th. N. Jersy. 11 Apr. 1863, typhoid, West's. "Sent home by M.P. Caull?".

HOYEN, CHAS. 8th. N.J. 22 Aug. 1862. M-315

HOYES, HENY. Co. B, 2nd. N.Y. 42 y/o. 9 Dec. 1862, ascites, West's. M-468

HOYT. GEORGE A. Co. H, 8th. Conn. 10 Sept. 1864, West's. M-975

HUBBARD, JOHN Co. I, 5th. N.C. C.S.A. 13 May 1862, Nat. Hotel. M-3

HUBBARD, T.J. Co. B, 7th. Tenn. C.S.A. 3 Aug. 1863, concussion. V-38

HUBBARD, THOMAS Co. H, 5th. N.J. 45 y/o. 20 Aug. 1862, Newton Univ. M-309

HUBER, JOHN Co. C, 2nd. Md. 23 Oct. 1862. M-7

HUFF, THOS. H. Co. D, 53rd. Pa. 26 Mar. 1864, pneumonia,. Camden St. Sent home.

HUGHES, JOHN Co. K, 49th. Pa. 26 y/o. 16 Dec. 1862, diarrhea, National. M-485

HULL, LEVI Co. K, 17th. Conn. 9 Dec. 1862, Calvert St. M-467

HULMES, JOSEPH Co. D, 8th. N.Y. Artl. 28 y/o. 14 Aug. 1863, drowned, Fed. Hill. M-698

HUNT, HENRY G. Co. K, 129th. N.Y. 1 Dec.(bur. 29 Nov.)1862. M-453

HUNT, WM. Co. L, 8th. New York. 18 y/o. 18 Sept. 1864, diarrhea, Jarvis.

HUNTING, ALVIN Co. I, 49th. N.Y. 20 y/o. 17 Sept. 1862, dyptheria, Patterson Park. M-343

HURD, FRANK W. Co. E, 12th. Mich. 17 y/o. 7 Jan. 1863, diarrhea, Nat. Hotel. M-535

HURGEN, MAXWELL Co. C, 83rd. Pa. Vol. 26 July 1862, typhoid. M-244

HURLBERT, FRANCIS Co. D, 86th. N.Y. 25 y/o. 12 June 1864, amputation of leg, Patterson. M-877

HUSK, FREDERICK Co. G, 85th. Pa. Vol. 26 y/o. 12 June 1862, typhoid, Nat. Hosp. M-156

HUSSEY, E.A. Co. I/J?, 12th. Mass. 21 Oct. 1862. M-400

HUTCHINSON, ALYNN Co. G, 137th. N.Y. 21 y/o. 7 Jan. 1863, pneumonia, West's. Sent home.

HUTCHINSON, SAML. Pvt. Co. A, 5th. Md. 27 y/o. 16 Mar. 1864, pneumonia, Camden St. M-189

HYDE, ALVIN Co. J, 3rd. Vt. 19 y/o. 7 Jan. 1863, pulmonalis, Nat. Hotel. M-528

HYLAND, AND. M. Co. D, 28th. Mass. 21 y/o. 18 Nov. 1862, typhoid, Stewart. M-393

IDENCH?, JOHN 2nd. Md. Regt. 24 y/o. 10 Dec. 1861, "congestion of the lungs". M-16

INGALLS, DAVID Co. D, 13th. S.C. C.S.A. 20 July 1863, Gunshot. M-40

IRONS, SEFHEUS Co. C, 121st. N.Y. 13 Aug. 1863. M-631

IRVING, CHARLES Co. G, 55th. N.Y. 17 May, 1862. M-98

ISSAMAN, MICHAEL Co. K, 61st. Pa. 60 y/o. 27 Aug. 1864, typhoid, Camden. M-966

JACKSON, AMASA Co. A, 4th. Maine. 11 Dec. 1862, Continental. M-473

JACKSON, HERMAN Co. I, 1st. Conn. Art. 17 y/o. 22 Sept. 1864, diarrhea, West's. M-1032

JACOBI, FELIX Co. H, 5th. N.Y. Art. 2 Aug. 1862. M-259

JAMES, JOHN Co. G, 45th. Ohio. 29 Apr. 1864, starvation at Richmond. M-832

JAMES, JOHN R. Co. E, 1st. Ma. Cavl. 30 Apr. 1862, mumps. M-89

JAMESON, DAVID A. Co. F, 2nd. U.S.S.Shooters. 26 y/o. 27 June 1864, gunshot, Patterson. M-1032

JARRETT, SAMUEL Co. C, 82nd. Ohio. 16 Sept. 1862, typhoid, Pat. Park. M-336

JOHNSON, FRANKLIN Pa. Art. 31 July 1862. M-266

JOHNSON, HARLEN S. Co. C, 2nd. Conn. H. Art. 27 y/o. 23 Sept. 1864, typhoid, National. M-1031

JOHNSON, ISAAC L. Co. A, 141st. Pa. 27 y/o. 16 July 1863, meningitis, Camden St.

JOHNSON, JOHN M. Co. C, 60th. Ohio. 18 y/o. 9 Oct. 1864, diarrhea. M-1063

JOHNSON, RICH'D. S. Co.A, 20th. Mich. 34 y/o. 23 Apr. 1863, phthisis, West's.

JOHNSTON, GEO. W. Co. K, 11th. Pa. Cavl. 6 Apr. 1864, pneumonia, Camden St. M-765

JOHNSTON, JAMES Co. B, 11th. Mass. 43 y/o. 5 July 1862, "gunshot at Williamsburg", Nat. Hotel Hosp. M-187

JOLINE, JOHN W. Co. I, 11th. N. Jersy. 19 y/o. 17 Aug. 1863, Jarvis. M-707

JOMETZ, JOHN 10 July 1863, lockjaw, West's Buildings. M-609

JONES, JAMES E. "Rebel" Co. C, 8th. Miss. 27 Apr. 1863, "wounded at Murfreesboro". V-39

JONES, JOHN Co. G, 8th. Va. 44 y/o. 17 July 1862, typhoid. M-224

JONES, LOUIS Co. A, 1st. Del. Cavl. 19 y/o. 8/?28 Apr. 1864, brain, Newton. M-823

JONES, OSCAR D. Co. M, 5th. N.Y. H. Artl. 27 y/o. 31 Aug. 1864, typhoid, Jarvis. M-980

JONES, THOMAS Co. H, 5th. N.C. C.S.A. 22 May 1862, gunshot, Nat. Hotel Hosp. Vault

JONES, THOMAS Substitute. 1 Oct., 1864, "shot attempting to escape the guard". M-1071

JONES, THORNTON Co. ?E, 70th. N.Y. 26 y/o. 20 Aug. 1863, Newton. M-708

JONES, WM. Co. F, 82nd. Ohio. 23 y/o. 26 July 1863, gunshot, Jarvis. M-668

JONES, WM. Co. I, 9th. Md. 40 y/o. 31 July 1863, "killed on railroad", Camden St. M-688

JONES, WILLIAM B. Co. G, 2nd. Tenn. 19 y/o. 13 May 1864. M-845

JOYBASS, ARAD Co. A, 26th. Mich. 17 y/o. 3 Mar. 1864, measles, Camden St. M-773

JUDGE, WM. Co. F, 33rd. Mass. 18 June 1863, "disease of the brain", McKim's. M-600

KAIN, JOHN Co. ?J, 3rd. Md. 9 Oct. 1862, Patterson Park. M-378

KANE, JOHN Co. E, 37th. N. York. 38 y/o. 3 July 1862, phlebitis, McKim's. M-182

KANNAN, WM. Co. G, 19th. N.Y. 9 July 1862. M-193

KANNER, SAMUEL Co. C, 86th. N. Y. 8 Dec. 1862. M-460

KATZ, ALEXANDER 19 May 1862, "Died on the way on the Steamer Vanderbilt". M-105

KAUFFMAN, J.M. Co. E, 107th. Pa. 22 y/o. 15 Oct. 1862, erysipelas, Newton. M-388

KEACH, STEPHEN W. Co. A, 10th. Md. 20 y/o. 6 Apr. 1862, pneumonia, Jarvis. M-809

KEARNEY, JOHN Co. C, 139th. N.Y. 50 y/o. 30 Oct. 1864, diarrhea, West's. M-1038

KEEGAN, ANDREW Co. B, 29th. Penna. Regt. 45 y/o. 30 Dec. 1861, typhoid, Nat. Hotel Hosp. M-20

KEEGAN, THOS. F. Co. B, 73rd. N.Y. 20 y/o. 5 Aug. 1863, gunshot, Jarvis. M-684

KEHOE, JOHN Pvt. Co. H, 1st. U.S. Art. 4 Dec. 1861, phthisis, Nat. Hotel Gen. Hosp. Sect. 12

KEIGHLEY, WM. Co. A, 29th. Maine. 32 y/o. 26 Aug. 1864, dysentery, Pat. Pk. M-983

KELL, THOMAS Co. B, 106th. N.Y. 34 y/o. 11 Oct. 1864, gunshot, Jarvis. M-1064

KELLEY, ANDREW J. Co. H, 1st. Md. Cavl. 35 y/o. 22 Apr. 1964, drowned, Camden St. M-786

KELLEY, HENRY P. Co. B, 1st. Del. Cavl. 46 y/o. 27 Oct. 1863, dysentey, Newton. M-740

KELLEY, ISAAC H. Co. A, 14th. Ind. 30 y/o. 26 July 1863, gunshot. M-692

KELLEY, JOHN B. Co. E, 29th. Pa. 10 Sept. 1862. M-329

KELLEY, JOHN F. Co. G, Maine Regt. 26 Sept. 1862. M-356

KELLEY, W.L. Co. E, 4th. Md. 11 Aug. 1862. M-292

KELLINGER, JOHN Co. D, 100th. N.Y. 11 June 1862, Pat. Park. M-149

KELLY, ALFRED Co. D, Purnell's Legion. 16 Apr. 1862. M-79

KELSEY, PHILIP Co. K, 4th. Ohio Cavl. 40 y/o. 8 July 1862, typhoid, Nat. Hotel. M-206

KEMP, PETER Co. C, 62nd. N.Y. 6 Aug. 1862. M-287

KENNEDY, CHARLES T. Co. H, 20th. Maine. 29 Nov. 1862, typhoid, McKim's. M-451

KENNEDY, JAMES Co. K, 168th. Pa. 22 y/o. 17 July 1863, typhoid, Nat. Hosp. M-624

KENNEDY, JAMES Co. K, 168th. Pa. 22 y/o. 17 July 1863, typhoid, Nat. Hotel. M-624

KENNEDY, JOHN Pvt. Co. I, 9th. N.Y. Regt. State Militia. 7 Dec. 1861, typhoid. M-13

KENNEDY, JOHN T. Co. K, 1st. Pa. Cavl. 26 July 1863, typhoid, Camden St. Sent home.

KENNESICK, MICHAEL Drum Major, 69th. N.Y. 34 y/o. 6 May 1864, typhoid, Camden St. M-829

KENYAN, W.W. Co. F, 1st. R.I. Artil. 25 y/o. 13th. Sept. 1864, West's. M-997

KERCHOFFER, CHARLES Sgt. Co. F, 5th. Va. Cav. 8 Aug. 1864. X?-917

KESSINGER, GEO. Co. D, 20th. N.Y. 22 y/o. 12 Jan. 1864, diarrhea, Continental. M-535

KESSLER, JAMES Pvt. 7th. Mich. Vol. 17 Apr. 1862, typhoid, Camden St. Hosp. M-93

?KEVETT, JOHN L. Co. H, 2nd. Tenn. Inf. 33 y/o. 18 May 1864, strangulated hernia. M-867

KEYES, MARION H. Co. H, 8th. Mich. 31 Mar. 1864, phthisis, Camden St. M-780

KEYSER, AUGUSTUS 32 y/o. 29 May 1862, typhoid, Nat. Hotel Hosp. M-132

KIMBALL, CHAS. H. Co. J?, 12th. Mass. 7 Oct. 1862. Sent home.

KINDRED, M.H. Co. E, 1st. E. Tenn. 28 y/o. 12 May 1864. M-842

KING, ALMIE Co. G, 5th. Va. 26 y/o. 23 Oct. 1864, pneumonia, Jarvis. M-1094

KING, C.A. Co. C, 129th. N.Y. 19 Nov. 1862. M-438

KING, GEORGE Co. E, 91st. N.Y. Vet. Vol. 33 y/o. 22 Oct. 1864, dysentry, Ft. Marshall. M-1192

KINGSBY, W. Co. A, 19th. Ind. 20 y/o. 3 Nov. 1862, typhoid, Nat. M-421

KINNEY, SILAS H. Co. K, 11th. N.Y. 23 Oct. 1862. M-408

KIRKLAND, JOHN Co. F, 1st. Mass. 26 y/o. 29 Dec.(d. 24 Dec.)1862, diarrhea, Newton. M-510

KIRKLAND, WM. F. 16th. N.Y. Cavl. 43 y/o. 14 May 1864, erysipelas, Camden St, M-843

KIRKWOOD, WM. Co. K/H?, 1st. Md. 26 July 1863, typhoid, West's. M-663

KITCH, DAVID C. Co. G, 10th. Pa. 19 y/o. 9 July 1862, typhoid, National. M-202

KITCHELL, ISAAC Co. A, 37th. N.Y. 33 y/o. 24 Jan. 1863, diarrhea, Newton. M-557

KITRIDGE, LOUIS Pvt. Co. D, 13th. Regt. Mass. Vol. 28 y/o. 23 Nov. 1861, typhoid fever, Nat. Hotel Hosp. M-1

KLINE, WM. Corp. 107th. Pa. Vol. 16 Oct. 1862. M-395

KLINE, WILLIAM 19 y/o. 18 oct. 1862, typhoid, Stewart's Mansion. M-395,

KLIPP, MELSHER Co. A, 91st. N.Y. 33 y/o. 23 Oct. 1864, manic potua?, Ft. Marshall. M-1083

KLOEN, WM. Co. F, 162nd. New York. 52 y/o. 21 Sept. 1864, diarrhea, Jarvis. M-977

KNAPP, G.G. Co. K, 42nd. Pa. 24 Sept. 1862, "died on Steamer Commodore". M-353

KOENIG, CHRISTIAN Co. B, 15th. N.J. Vol. 20 y/o. 27 Oct. 1864, gunshot wound, Nat. M-1140

KOHL, PETER Co. B, 1st. N.Y. 7 Jan. 1862, congestive fever, Nat. Hotel Hosp. M-35

KOLP, JOHN Co. K, 47th. Pa. 49 y/o. 22 Oct. 1864, hemoroids, Jarvis. M-1078

KRALL, CHRISTIAN Co. K, 120th. Pa. 43 y/o. 6 Jan. 1862, gunshot, Stewart's Mansion. M-527

KRUZER, CHARLES Co. G, 16th. Mich. 38 y/o. 24 May 1864, gunshot, Patterson. M-863

KUHN, GEORGE Co. K, 2nd. Md. 53 y/o. 18 Nov. 1862, dysentery, Nat. M-436

KUNKEL, JOHN W. Co. H, 141st. Pa. 18 y/o. 5 Aug. 1863, gunshot, Jarvis. M-639

LAMISON, GEO. Co. C, 110th. Pa. 25 y/o. 3 Aug. 1863, gunshot, West's. M-670

LAMPSON, SYLVESTER Co. A, 2nd. Conn. 18 y/o. 25 Oct. 1864, typhoid, Newton. M-1014

LAMUSON?, E.R. Co. D, 13th. Ind. 41 y/o. 25 Nov. 1862, pulmonalis, Stewart's. M-446

LANCASTER, BARTHOLOMEW Co. E, 140th. Pa. 20 y/o. 30 Dec.(d. 22 Dec.) 1862, Nat. Hotel. M-513

LANCASTER, W.T. Co. F, 3rd. Va. C.S.A. 30 y/o. 11 Aug. 1863, gunshot wound. V-38, grave 54.

LANGLEY, GEO. W. Co. J?, 59th. Mass. 18 y/o. 25 July 1864, typhoid fever, Patterson. M-934

LANKFORD, DAVID E. Co. G, 1st. Eastern Shore Md.. 23 y/o. 1 June 1864, gunshot, Lafayette Square. M-807

LAN_SHIRE, EDW. Pvt. Co. J, 28th. N.Y.S. Vol. 20 Nov. 1861, typhoid fever, U.S.A. Hosp., Nat. Hotel. M-2. body #7.

LANTZ, DANIEL Co. H, 1st. Mass. 25 y/o. 24 Jan. 1863, ?drowning, Nat. Hotel. M-554

LATIMER, EDWARD H. 2nd. Lt. Co. C, Ct. Cavl. 23 y/o. 14 Feb. 1864, hemorrhage, Camp Cheeseborough. M-802

LATOWN, THOS. Co. E, 27th. Ind. 10 Jan. 1862. M-39

LAWRENCE, J.E. Sgt. Co. H, 111th. N.Y. 35 y/o. 22 July 1863, gunshot, West's. Sent home.

LAWRENCE, LAWSON J. Co. C, 2nd. Mass. 21 y/o. gunshot wound, National. M-1080

LAWSON, C.M. Co. K, 50th. Va. C.S.A. 19 Oct. 1864. V-?

LAWSON, CHANCEL Co. C, 27th. Mass. 48 y/o. 16 Sept. 1864, diarrhea, West's. M-1013

LAWSON, JAMES Co. F, 111th. Pa. Vol. 30 Apr. 1862, measles. M-90

LAWSON, JOHN M. (?John McLawson) Co. C, 3rd. Md. 9 May 1862. M-96

LAWSON, NELSON Co. D, 5th. N.Y. Artl. 23 June 1862, gunshot. M-173

LAWSON, S. Co. E, 22nd. Ga. C.S.A. 41 y/o. 6 Sept. 1863, gunshot. V-37

LEAR, JOSEPH Co. A, 5th. Vt. 22 y/o. 6 Jan.(d. 31 Dec.)1863, diarrhea, Nat. M-525

LEAVER, JAMES H. Co. A, 22nd. Pa. Cavl. 24 y/o. 5 May 1864, starvation at Richmond, Jarvis. M-837

LEECH, JOHN A. Co. B, 23rd. Pa. 21 y/o. 3 Dec. 1862, diarrhea, West's. "Put in Haggerty's grave", M-233

LEECH. W.W. Co. S, 134th. Pa. 21 Jan. 1863, asphyxia, McKim's. M-547, sent home. "Alex Fox put in his place".

LEHMAN, DAVITT Co. G, 134th. N.Y. 19 y/o. 9 Oct. 1862, typhoid, National Hospital. M-377

LELAND, THOMAS Co. A, 11th. Maine. 4 June 1862, typhoid, National Hotel. M-155

LESPITE, EDWD. Co. A, 3rd. Md. Cavl. 1 Nov.(d. 31 Oct.)1863, diarrhea, Patterson. M-743

LESTER, JONATHAN J. 5th. N.C. C.S.A. Died 27 May 1862, gunshot wound of ankle, National. In vault.

LEVEVEY, James A. Co. H, 26th. Va. C.S.A. 21 Oct. 1864. V-?

LEVITT, ALPHEA L. Co. C, 20th. Maine. 24 y/o. 27 Jan. 1863. typhoid fever, Patterson Park. M-598

LEWIS, DAVID S. 19 May 1862, "d. on the Steamer Vanderbilt". M-106

LEWIS, G.S. Co. H, 4th. Va. C.S.A. 18 Oct. 1864. V-?

LEWIS, SHRODER Co. F, 8th. Va. Regt. 25 y/o. 26 Sept. 1862, M-357

LIEDEMAN, EARNST Co. H, 20th. Mich. Vol. 22 Mar. 1863, typhoid ("d. on his way from Newport News"), West Hosp. M-579

LIGHT, GEO. W. Co. H, 14th. Va. C.S.A. 16 July 1863. M-40

LILLOCK, L.C. Co. F, 12th. Regulars. 17 y/o. 9 July 1862, "prostantis",. M-199

LINCOLN, HERBERT L. Co. A, 35th. Mass. 13 Oct. 1862, vulnus schoph, Newton Hosp. M-385

LINES, JESSE Co. K, 81st. Pa. 25 y/o. 9 Jan. 1864, typhoid, Newton. M-735

LINFIELD, LEVI Soldier. Co. A, 5th. Pa. 22 July 1862. M-234

LIVENZEY, JOHN Co. B, Purnell's Legion. 24 y/o. 18 Feb. 1862, pneumonia, Adams House Hosp. M-56

LOCHER, PROSPER Co. K, 98th. N.Y. 19 y/o. Nat. Canada. 16 July 1862, diarrhea, National. M-223

LOCKLIN, GEO. N. Co. I, 2nd. Conn. 20 y/o. 21 Oct. 1864, typhoid, Jarvis. Sent home.

LOCKWOOD, DAVID Co. K, 11th. Va. 13 Oct. 1864, typhoid, Jarvis. M-1068

LODER, JAMES G. Co. A, 4th. Pa. Vol. 10 Aug. 1863. M-677

LONG, FRANK Co. L, 5th. U.S? Artl. 6 Jan. 1863. M-523

LOUIS, GARDNER Co. B, 19th. Ind. 22 y/o. 24 Dec. 1863, gunshot, Jarvis. M-749

LOURY. WILLIAM Co. E, 70th. N.Y. 5 June 1862, februs remict,_ _, Patterson Park. M-158

LOWDER, CHARLES Co. G, 3rd. N.J. 33 y/o. 20 Oct. 1864, diarrhea, Jarvis. M-1100

LOWE, HILERY Co. A, 2nd. Tenn. 21 y/o. 22 June 1864, starvation, Jarvis. M-882

LOWELL, ELLBRIDGE A. Co. G, 20th. Maine. 13 Dec. 1862, typhoid. M-477

LOWELL, JAMES E. Co. C, 17th. Mass. 11 Feb. 1862. M-54

LUCLAY, JOHN Co. G, 3rd. Mass. Regt. 23 y/o. 29 Sept. 1864, debility, National. M-1037

LUDDINGTON, L.S. Co. A, 2nd. Conn. 33 y/o. 21 Oct. 1864, typhoid, Jarvis. M-928

LYONS, _ _ Soldier. 25 July 1862. M-242

MACE, GEORGE Co. A, 17th. Mass. Regt. Camp Andrews. 23 Dec. 1861. M-?

MACK, JNO. M. Pvt. Co. D, 11th. Capt. Price. Apr. 1862, McKim's Mansion. M-82

MACKEN, JAMES Co. A, 69th. N.Y.S.M. 4 June 1862, "d. of injuries rec'd on way to Balt. R. Road", Camden St. Hosp. M-154

MADDEN, WILLIAM Co. I, 57th. Pa. 4 June 1864, "d. typhoid at Patterson Park", "was to have M-156 but was sent home before being sent to cemetery".

MAHAN, JOHN Co. K, 13th. Pa. Cavl. 32 y/o. 18 May 1863, "d. at U. Relief". M-591

MANGER, JOHN 66th? Ohio. 18 Sept. 1862. M-341

MANLEY, JOHN Co. E, 100th. N.Y. Regt. 26 May 1862. M-122

MANNING, TOBIAS 5th. N.C. C.S.A. 17 May 1862, gunshot, National Hosp. Vault

MARBECK, ANTON Co. C, 75th. Pa. Vol. 39 y/o. 6 Sept. 1863, gangrene, Jarvis Hosp. M-318

MARLEN, JOHN Co. A, 10th. N.Y. Cavl. 30 July 1862, heart disease. M-264

MARTIN, E.O. Co. D, 11th. Tenn. 4 Apr. 1864, "Paroled prisoner, died on the way", Camden St. M-821.

MARTIN, FREDERICK Co. D, 1st. Md. Cavl. Regt. 44 y/o. 9 Nov. 1861, strangulation, "died at No. 261 Ann St". M-6, body # 2

MARTIN, FREDK. Co. H, 7th. N.Y. 31 y/o. 22 Dec.(d. 16 Dec.)1862, pulmonalis, National. M-504

MARTIN?, JOHN Co. C, 30th. N.Y. 38 y/o. 26 Dec. 1862, pneumonia, Continental. M-506

MARTIN, THOMAS 2nd. Batl. V.R.C., 72nd. Co. 3 Aug. 1864, gastritis, Newton. M-931

MARTIN, WALTER Co. C, 2nd. Md. 27 Dec. 1861, typhoid. M-23

MARTIN, WM. Co. C, 11th. Pa. R.C. 18 Sept. 1862, gunshot, Nat. Hosp. M-345

MARTINSON, JAMES Co. A, 57th. Pa. 23 Aug. 1862, typhoid. M-316

MASH, JAMES Co. D, 8th. Va. 45 y/o. 18 July 1862, phthisis, National. M-214

MASON, DANIEL Co. C, 1st. Del. Cavl. 26 y/o. 9 Sept. 1863, typhoid fever, Newton Univ. M-729

MASON, EDWARD Co. K, 60th. N.Y. 6 Feb. 1862. M-51

MASTEN. MICHAEL Co. A, 9th. N.Y.H.A. 25 y/o. 17 July 1864, gunshot. M-894

MATTHEWS, WM. F. 59th. N.Y., Hosp. Steward. 40 y/o. 6 Feb. 1864, delirium tremens, Jarvis. M-642

MAXFIELD, DANIEL Co. G, 19th. Mass. 28 y/o. 24 June 1864, consumption, Patterson. M-879

MAXWELL, DAVIS Co. C, 129th. N.Y. 29 y/o. Sent home.

MAYER, ALBERT Co. E, 6th. U.S. Cavl. 25 y/o. 25 May 1863, National. M-592

McALLISTER, M. Co. H, 57th. Pa. 13 Sept. 1862, diarrhea, McKim's. M-333

McBAIN, WM. Co. E, 23rd. Ill. Regt. 31 y/o. 25 Sept. 1864, Patterson. M-1029

McCABE, THO. Co. A, Balt. Lt. Inf. 10 Apr. 1862. M-74

McCALLAM, SAMUEL F. Co. B, 76th. Pa. Vol. 10 Dec. 1861, typhoid, Nat. Hotel Hosp. M-15

McCASKILL, DANIEL Co. H, 26th. N.C. C.S.A. 24 y/o. 20 Nov. 1863. V-37

MCCAUSLAND, ALONZO Co. J, 16th. Maine. 19 y/o. 17 Dec. 1862, pulmonalis. M-492

McCLAY, JOHN Co. E, 106th. Penn. 7 Jan. 1862, lungs, National. M-533

McCLENNEN, SYLVESTER Co. H, 20th. Maine. 13 Dec. 1862. M-471

McCOLN, SAM'L. K. Co. E, 91st. Ohio. 27 y/o. 11 Aug. 1864, typhoid fever, Jarvis. M-919

McCONNELL, PATRICK Co. I/J?, 4th. N.Y. 21 y/o. 15 Oct. 1863, gunshot, National. M-391

McCORMICK, JOHN Co. D, 4th. Ma. 16 Dec. 1862. M-487

McCOY, SAMUEL Co. M, 16th. Ill. Cavl. 22 Apr. 1864, diarrhea, West's. M-789

McDANNEL, WM. Co. E, 72nd. Pa. 7 Aug. 1863, West's. M-645

McDEVITT, EDWARD Co. D, 82nd. N.Y. 13 Dec. 1862, diarrhea, Patterson Park. M-478

McDEVITT, WM. Co. K, Purnell's Legion. 25 Apr. 1862. M-87

McDONALD, JOHN 5th. N.Y. Artl. 4 Sept. 1862. M-194

McDOWELL, JAMES H. Co. L, 3rd. N.Y. Cavl. 24 Mar. 1862, typhoid, Camden St. Hosp. M-76

McELHANEY, SAMUEL Co. C, 4th. Pa. Cavl. 19 y/o. 28 May 1864, diarrhea. M-866

McGUIRE, ALEX Co. H, 6th. Ky. Cavl. 25 Apr. 1864, diarrhea, West's. M-818

McGUIRE, GEO. Co. H, 5th. N.Y.H.A. 22 y/o. 18 Sept. 1864, typhoid, Patterson. M-1048

McINTYRE, DAVID Co. B, 14th. Conn. Vol. 23 Apr. 1864, diarrhea, M-797

McKEINE, MELVIN Pvt. Co. D, 4th. Wisc. 26 Jan. 1862. M-45

McKENSIE, ROBERT Co. F, 24th. N. York. 31 y/o. 15 May 1863, killed on railroad, Nat. Hotel Hosp. M-596

McKINSEY, CHAS. H. Co. F, 6th. Maine. 23 Feb. 1862, typhoid, Nat. Hotel Hosp. M-64

McKLUSKY, JOHN Co. A, 5th. Maine. 18 y/o. 7 Feb. 1863, typhoid, National. M-563

McKUSICK, JAS. S. Co. D, 20th. Maine. 24 y/o. 15 Dec. 1862, typhoid, National. M-486

McKUSICK, JAS. S. Co. D, 20th. Maine. 24/6? y/o. 15 Dec.1862, typhoid, National. M-542

McLAUGHLIN TIMOTHY Co. M, 2nd. Ill. Artl. 22 Apr. 1864, diarrhea and starvation, West's. M-790

McLAUGHLIN, TIMOTHY M. Paroled Prisoner. Co. M, 2nd. Ill. Artl. 22 Apr. 1864, diarrhea & starvation, Wests. M-790

McLAWSON, JOHN? Co. C, 3rd. Md. 9 May 1862. M-96

McLAWSON, JOHN Co. C, 3rd. Md. 9 May 1862. M-96

McLEAN, J. 27 Jan. 1863, drowned. M-553

McLINCH, EDWARD H. Co. D, 2nd. Regt. N.Y. 18 y/o. 15 July 1863, gunshot, Newton. M-650

McMULLEN, WM. H./JAMES? Co. I, 106th. Penn. Vol. 25 Mar. 1862, meningitis, Camden St. M-75

McNALLAY, PETER Soldier. 3 Aug. 1862. M-270

McNAULTY, JAMES Co. B, 1st. Mass. 40 y/o. 4 Sept. 1863, dropsy, Jarvis. M-733

McNEIL, WM. Co. C, 4th. U.S. Artl. 23 y/o. 18 July 1863, shell wound, Newton's. M-649

MEARING, M.S. Co. A, 15th. N.C. Cavl. 22 y/o. 10 Aug. 1864, Jarvis. M-927

MEGARGA, JOSEPH Recruit. 18 y/o. 16 Aug. 1864, "killed", Camden St. M-938

MENBERGER, JOHN J. Co. D, 1st. Md. Cavl. 1 June 1864, drowned, Camden St. M-792

MERCER, JAMES B. Co. G, 3rd. Md. 47 y/o. 12 July 1864, pneumonia. M-938

MEREDITH, JOHN Co. B, 49th. Pa. 22 y/o. 31 Dec. 1862, diarrhea, West's. M-516

MERRELL, C.H. Co. F, 2nd. Conn. Art. 21 y/o. 22 Oct. 1864, Jarvis. M-1172

MERRELL, LEWIS W. Co. K, 7th. Maine. 22 y/o. 9 Dec. 1862, diarrhea, Nat. Hotel. M-464

METZELL, ALEX 26th. Wisc. 28 y/o. 21 July 1863, tyemia?, Camden St. M-638

MICKELSON, JAMES Co. G, 22nd. Wisc. 21 June 1863, diarrhea, Ft. Masters. M-599

MIDKIFF, WM. Co. C, 8th. Va. 23 y/o. 17 Feb. 1863, typhoid, West's. M-574

MILES, BENJ. Co. B, 12th. N.J. 53 y/o. 27 Jan. 1863, Nat. Sent home.

MILES, JAMES L. Co. B, 143rd. Penna. 32 y/o. 5 Aug. 1863, gunshot, West's. M-683

MILIKEN, RICHARD Pvt. Co. K, 4th. Wisc. Regt. Cavl. 24 Nov. 1861, typhoid fever, Nat. Hotel. Hosp. M-9, body #2

MILLARD, RICH'D Co. B, 77th. N.Y. 40 y/o. 11 Dec. 1862, dropsy on brain, National. Sent home.

MILLER, IRA Co. E, 7th. Md. 25 y/o. 13 sept. 1862, debility, Frederick. M-334

MILLER, JOHN the 1st. Co. I, ?1st. Ma. Cavl. 26 Apr. 1862, killed on the railroad. M-88

MILLER, JOHN Co. A, 4th. N. Jersy. 29 July 1962. M-259

MILLER, M.G. Co. F, 87th. N.Y. 23 y/o. 14 Oct. 1862, marasmus, Newton. M-389

MILLER, ?MANA Co. G, 128th. Pa. 7 Dec. 1862. M-373

MILLER, MILTON Co. C, 1st. Pa. 29 July 1862. M-254

MILLER, PETER C. Co. J, 1st. N.Y. Artl. 28 y/o. 13 July 1862, typhoid. M-213

MILLS, H.H. Co. D, 24th. Mich. 23 y/o. 19 Oct. 1863, diarrhea, Union R. Rooms. M-735

MILLS, I.C. Pvt. Co. F, 1st. Pa. 30 Dec. 1861, typhoid, Nat. M-29

MILLS, THOS. A. 1st. Leut. Co. E, 4th. Ma. 30 y/o. 26 Aug. 1864, "killed at Reams Station". A-119

MIMS, JOHN K. Co. E, 1th. Miss. C.S.A. 24 y/o. 13 Mar. 1864, gunshot wound. V-37

MINARD, LEONARD E. Co. C, 17th. Mich. 19 y/o. 30 Dec. (d. 27 Dec.) 1862, vulnus sclopt, Nat. M-517

MITCHELL, HOLLEY E. Co. K, 60th. N.Y. 1 Jan. 1861. Permit from Meyer Belger. M-31

MITCHELL, JOHN B. Co. E, 20th. Maine. 23 y/o. 1 Nov. 1862, typhoid. M-430, sent home

MOLIDOR, GEO. Co. C, 52nd. N.Y. 9 June 1862, typhoid, Pat. Park M-146 MOLLERS, MATTISON Co. H, 8th. Va. 8 Aug. 1862, typhoid. M-284

MONCKTON, EDWARD Co. E, 96th. Pa. 34 y/o. 17 July 1862, ?chronice, National. M-225

MOODY, MARSHALL Co. C, 84th. Pa. 22 July 1863, typhoid, West's. M-632

MOON, SAMUEL Co. B, 57th. N.Y. Artl. 28 y/o. 19 Nov. 1863. M-615

MOORE, AARON Co. A, 5th. N.C. C.S.A. 24 May 1862, National Hotel Hosp. Vault

MOORE, CHARLES Co. D, 42nd. N.Y. 38 y/o. 6 Sept. 1863, hemorrhage, Jarvis. M-727

MOORE, FREDERICK Co. K, 14th. Conn. 22 y/o. 3 June 1864, starvation & diarrhea. M-871

MOORE, GEORGE Co. C, 96th. N.Y. 11 June 1862, typhoid, Patterson Park Gen. Hosp. M-153

MOORE, JERVIS Co. J, 134th. N.Y. 19 y/o. 13 Oct. 1862, typhoid, National. M-389

MOORE, JOHN Co. E, 105th. N.Y. 33 y/o. 13 Dec. 1862, pulmonalis, Stewart's. M-481

MOORE, JOHN C. Co. F, 2nd. New Hampshire. 18 y/o. 22 July 1863, gunshot, Jarvis. M-636

MOORE, JOS. Co. F, 129th. N.Y. 19 Nov. 1862. M-437

MOORE, MANVILLE Co. G, 8th. Ohio. 23 y/o. 15 July 1863, gunshot, McKim's. "Sent home by Wheeler".

MOORE, WM. Co. D, 100th. N.Y. 11 Aug. 1862, heart disease. M-294

MORBRAY, J.E. Co. G, 52nd. N.C. C.S.A. 27 July 1863. M-38

MORGAN, DANIEL F. Co. K, 8th. Mass. 18 y/o. 10 Aug. 1864. M-930, sent home.

MORLEY, JOHN Co. F, 170th. N.Y. 34 y/o. 6 Nov. 1862, pulmonalis. M-427

MORRIS, EDM. H. Co. I/T?, 20th. Ind. 18 y/o. 25 Oct. 1862, dysentery. M-414

MORRISON, JOSEPH Co. H, 87th. Ohio. 7 July 1862, gunshot accident. M-195

MORRISON, SCOTT Co. B, 36th. Mass. 26 Mar. 1863, West's Hosp. M-581

MOULTON, DANIEL Co. D, 6th. N.Y. Artl. 32 y/o. 5 Sept. 1863. pneumonia, Jarvis. M-725

MOUNTS/MOULNS, JAMES Co. D, 106th. Pa. Vol. 30 y/o. 23 July 1862, typhoid, National Hotel. M-237

MOUREY, HENRY B. Co. B, 6th. Pa. Vol. 37 y/o. 30 Sept. 1862, gunshot. M-362

MUCKRIDGE, WM. Co. E, 10th. Regt. N.Y. 24 y/o. 16 Aug. 1862, typhoid, National Hotel. M-301

MULLENS, HENRY C. Co. F, 150th. N.Y. 25 y/o. 1 June 1863, typhoid, Camden St. M-221

MULLINS, GEO. Co. A, 9th. N.Y.H.A. 58 y/o. 16 Sept. 1864, dysentery, Jarvis. M-1015

MULLINS, GEO. Co. K, 8th. Pa. 29 July 1862. M-261

MUNGO, E.M. Co. K, 6th. S.C. Inf. C.S.A. 23 Oct. 1864, diarrhea. Sect. V, grave 94

MUNNS, WM. Mc. Co. B, ?43/63rd. Penna. 4 Aug. 1862. M-278

MUNSON, MARCUS Co. K, 1st. Conn. Cavl. 18 y/o. 12 Mar. 1864, pneumonia, Jarvis. M-772

MURDOCK, DENNIS Co. A, 111th. Pa. Regt. Capt. Burley. 25 Apr. 1862. M-86

MURRAY, ARTHUR Co. B, 2nd. N.Y. Cavl. 21 y/o. 12 Sept. 1864, gunshot, Camden St. M-1009

MURRAY, SAMUEL Co. C, 6th. N.Y. 20 y/o. 24 Sept. 1862, gunshot, National. M-345

MYERS, AMBROSE Co. A, 52nd. Pa. Vol. 30 y/o. 27 June 1862, pneumonia, Stewart's Mansion. M-177

MYERS, HENRY W. 72nd. N.Y. Regt. 25 y/o. 17 May 1862, gunshot. M-97, body disinterred.

NARNEY/VARNEY?, JACOB W. Co. F, 161st. Ohio, 19 y/o. 4 Oct. 1864, typhoid fever, Patterson Park. M-1055

NASH, FRANK 13th. Pa. Cavl. 19 Apr. 1864, "died on the boat", West's. M-799

NAUGHTON, JOHN Co. H, 11th. Maine. 20 May 1862. M-110

NE/I/U?RNEY, I. Rebel soldier. 14 May 1862. M-4

NELLING, JOHN W. Co. K, 1st. Mass. 26 Aug. 1862. M-317

NELSON, JOHN Co. G, 49th. N.Y. 20 y/o. 18 Nov. 1862, diarrhea, Newton. M-434

NEUBLING, FREDK. C. Co. B, 26th. Mich. 22 y/o. 15 Apr. 1863, West's. M-589

NEWCOMB, THOMAS B. Co. M, 11th. Vt. 26 y/o. 4 Oct. 1864, typhoid fever, Patterson Park. M-1056

NEWTON, GEO. D. Pvt. Co. B, 2nd. Mass. 30 Dec. 1861, typhoid, National Hotel Hosp. M-28, "body was disinterred and sent home. Geo. W. Woodson was put in this grave".

NICHOLS, ALANSON Co. F, 157th. N.Y. 11 June 1864, Jarvis. M-872

NICKOLSON, WM. N. Co. B, Purnell's Legion. 24 y/o. 30 Sept. 1862, typhoid. M-345

NIM?, MORGAN Co. I, 145th. Pa. 20 July 1863, gunshot. M-664

NIVEN, HENRY Co. D, Stockton's Ind. Rifles. 1 Nov. 1861, typhoid, National Hosp. M-1, body #2

NIXON, JESSEE B. Co. C, W. Va. Militia. 23 Apr. 1864, bronchitis, West's. M-796

NOBLE, JOHN Co. C, 60th. Ohio. 24 June 1864, gunshot, Patterson. M-881

NORMAN, RUDOLPH Co. G, 28th. Mass. 5 June 1864, diarrhea and starvation. M-859

NORTON, MARTIN Co. I, 73rd. N.Y. 23 y/o. 31 July 1863. M-671

NOWLAND, JOHN Co. C, 53rd. Pa. 3 Aug. 1862. M-272

NOY, EDW. Co. F, 11th. Ky. Cavl. 20 Apr. 1864, diarrhea, West's. M-801

NOYES, CHARLES M. Co. E, 2nd. Vermont. 23 y/o. 22 Oct. 1862, typhoid, National. M-405

NOYES, G.H. Co. D, 11th. Maine. 25 y/o. 10 July 1862, typhoid, National. M-204

OAKLEY, RICHARD Co. A, 8th. Pa. R.C. 21 July 1862. M-243

O'BRIAN, WM. Co. D, 28th. Mass. 19 y/o. 13 Dec. 1862, typhoid, Stewart's. M-430

O'CONNOR, ROBERT Co. C, 70th. N.Y. 30 y/o. 22 July 1863, gunshot, Jarvis. M-626

ODELL, LEO Co. G, 56th. N.Y. 15 Aug. 1862. M-30

OGLETREE, B.F. Co. I, 13th. Ga. C.S.A. 37 y/o. 24 Aug. 1864. V-36

OLIVER, JAMES W. Co. A, 116th. Ohio. 40 y/o. 2 Oct. 1864, diarrhea, Patterson Park. M-070

OLLIVER, SAMUEL Co. E, 81st. Pa. 27 May 1862. M-125

?OLUNUCH, DANIEL Co. D, 1st. Md. 6 Nov. 1862. M-426

O'NEIL, PATRICK C. Co. K, 2nd. Batt., 22nd. Regt. 24 y/o. 6 Mar. 1864, Newton. M-778

ORNSBY, JAMES 11 Apr. 1863, Ft. Masters. M-590

ORTT, JACKSON H. Co. I, 104th. Pa. 30 May 1862, Patterson Park. M-138

OSBORNE, J.M. Co. A, 14th. La. C.S.A. 25 July 1863. V-?

OSBOURNE, JAMES Pvt. 1st. Md. Regt. Cavl. 23 y/o. 26 Nov. 1861, intermittant fever, National. Grave #10. body #1

OSBOURNE, JOHN Co. D, 59th. N.Y. 24 y/o. 22 Dec. (d. 15 Dec.) 1862, dysentery, National. M-495

O'SHEA, DANIEL Co. E, 42nd. N.Y. 26 July 1863, gunshot, West's. M-635, sent home by brother.

OSTEEN, STEPHEN Co. B, 1st. Md. Cavl. 23 Feb. 1862. M-59

OSTRANDER, H.L. Co. B, 5th. Mich. Cavl. 22 Apr. 1864, "starvation at Richmond", Jarvis. M-788, sent home.

OWEN, J.P. Miss. Regt. C.S.A. 21 Apr. 1864, "killed". V-?

OWENS, L.B. Sgt. Co. E, 1st. Conn, Artl. 31 July 1862. M-269

OYER, ELIJAH Co. H, 147th. N.Y. 21 y/o. 1 Jan. 1863, typhoid, Stewart's. M-548

PAGE, CHRISTIAN Co. D, 101st. Pa. 27 June 1862, typhoid, Patterson Park. M-178

PAGE, GEO. S. Co. F, 25th. Mass. 24 y/o. 26 June 1864, gunshot wound, West's. Sent home

PALMER, JAMES Co. D, 146th. N.Y. 21 y/o. 21 July 1863, Jarvis. M-696

PANOUSHI, JACOB Co. G, 4th. U.S. Artl. 19 Aug. 1862. M-300

PARK, WM. Co. H, 149th Ohio. 37 y/o. 27 June 1864, typhoid fever, Jarvis. M-935

PARKER, DANIEL 49th. Regt. Penn. Vol., Col. Irvine. 22 y/o. b. Pa. 28 Sept. 1861, "killed on the R.R.". DD-63

PARKER, LEWIS L. 6 Dec. 1862, Calvert St. Hosp. M-462

PARKINSON, EDW. 9th. N.Y. 28 y/o. 9 Dec. 1961, typhoid, Nat. Hotel Hosp. M-14

PARSONS, JOHN Co. C, Mass. Battery. 31 July 1862. M-262

PATTERSON, CHARLES S. Co. H, 6th. Maine. Sept. 1862, typhoid, Patterson Park. M-344

PATTERSON, HENRY Co. D, 157th. N.Y. 7 Feb. 1863. M-565

PATTERSON, JOB Co. D, 8th. N.J. 27 May 1867, "wounded at Williamsburg", National. M-126

PAUL, BERTRAND Co. H, 188th. Pa. 21 y/o. 15 Sept. 1864, remittant fever, West's. M-1000

PAXTON, ALBERT Co. B, 84th. N.Y. 10 Sept. 1862, "died in Aug., unbalanced". M-326

PAYNE, E.J. Sgt. Co. B, 5th. N.Y. Art. 30 Oct. 1863, typhoid. M-742

PEAK, WM. N. Co. C, 19th. Wis. 18 y/o. 15 Sept. 1864, typhoid fever, West's. M-1008

PEASE, _ _ Co. B, 37th. Mass. Regt. 2 J_ 186_, typhoid, Newton Hosp. M-604

PENBECK, LYMON H. 1st. N.Y. Cavl. 31 Aug. 186?, Ft. Fed. Hill. M-969

PE_VEY, JOHN L. Co. D, 5th. N. Hampshire. 3 Aug. 1862. M-274

PERKINS, A.N. Co. K, 2nd. Conn. H.A. 38 y/o. 13 Aug. 1864, gunshot wound, Patterson. M-925

PERKINSON, ROBERT H. Co. B, "Hoods Batt'n.". CSA 14 Oct. 1864. V-?

PETERS, MICHAEL Co. D, 56th. Pa. 51 y/o. 6 Nov. 1863, pneumonia, Camden St. M-744

PETERSON, SILAS N. Co. D, 38th. Mass. 25 y/o. 13 Sept. 1862, typhoid, Stewart's. M-475

PFAFF, GOTTLEIB Co. C, 111th. Pa. 24 June 1862, diarrhea. M-172

PFEFFERMAN, VALDIN? Co.A, Purnell's Legion. 58 y/o. b. Bavaria. 3 June 1862. M-149

PHILLIPS, BENAMIN Co. E, 5th. Fla. C.S.A. 14 Oct. 1864. V-?

PHILLIPS, LORENZO Co. E, 126th. N.Y. 13 July 1863, hem., West's. M-614

PHILLIPS, PATRICK Co. C, 99th. Pa. 23 May 1864, "gunshot at Spotsylvanis". M-857

PIERCE, J.K. Co. M, 5th. N.Y. H. Artl. 24 y/o. 22 Oct. 1864, bronchitis, Jarvis. M-1125

PIKE, GEORGE Co. F, 111th. Pa. 18 y/o. 17 Mar. 1862. M-72

PLASMAN, HENRY Co. H, 98th. Pa. 20 Sept. 1862. M-346

POLE, CHARLES Co. D, 151st. N.Y. 13 Jan. 1862. M-522

POPE, D.E. Co. I, Holcombe, S.C. Legion. 14 Oct. 1864, "dead when brought to the hospital". V-?

PORTER, EDWIN H. Pvt. Co. H, 60th. N.Y. 9 Jan. 1862. M-41, disinterred 11 Feb. 1862.

POTTER, DAVID Co. C, Ohio Cavl. 4 Aug. 1862. M-275

POUCHOR, JOHN G. CO. K, 14th. Pa. 29 y/o. 24 Aug. 1864, typhoid, Camden St. M-950

POULL, ISAAC Co. K, 17th. Pa. Cavl. 16 y/o. July 1863, diarrhea, Camden St. M-665

POWERS, EDWIN Co. H, 7th. Ind. 23 y/o. 6 Sept. 1863, diarrhea, McKims. M-721

PRATT, LUTHER L. Soldier. 4 Aug. 1862, National Hotel. M-279

PRENT ICE, SIDNEY Co. H, 7th. Mich. Cavl. 49 y/o. 25 Sept. 1864, diarrhea, McKim's. M-1043

PRESCOTT, ELISHA Co.A, 100th. Ohio. 28 Apr. 1864, diarrhea, West's. M-814

PRESTON, CHARLES Sgt. 3rd. Md. Regt. 25 y/o. 12 July 1862, typhoid. M-210

PRESTON, EDWIN Co. D, 5th. N.Y. 20 y/o. 25 Oct. 1864, typhoid, Jarvis. M-1085

PRESTON, GEO. Co. H, 2nd. Mass. Vol. 37 y/o. 24 June 1862, hepatitis, National Hotel.

PRESTON,JAMES Co. D, 2nd. U.S. Artl. 34 y/o. 21 Aug. 1864, diarrhea, Camden St. M-949

PRICE, FREDK. J. Co. D, 10th. Ma. 11 July 1863, Ft. Masters. M-612

PRICE?, G.W. Co. H, 55th. Ohio. 19 y/o. 23 Dec.(d. 19 Dec.)1862, pulmonalis, National. M-502

PRICE, HUGH Va. C.S.A. 11 May 1864, diarrhea. V-36

PRICE, ISAAC W. Leut. 63rd. Pa. 29 Aug. 1864, Camden St. Sent home.

PRINCE, HENRY L. Co. F, 7th. Maine. 18 y/o. 26 Oct. 1864, gunshot wound, Jarvis. M-1087

PUCKET, LEWIS Co. C, 126th. Ohio. 45 y/o. 28 July 1864, bronchitis. M-897

PUTMAN, JAMES Co. B, 2nd. U.S. Cavl. 21 y/o. 20 Aug. 1864, februs remittant, Patterson Park. M-944

QUINLEY, PVT. 8th. U.S. Inf. 24 Sept. 1862, "killed on railroad". M-352

RABER, H.L. Co. A, 8th. Va. CSA 14 Aug. 1863, gunshot wound. M-38

RANKINS, WILLIAM Co. J, 170th. Ohio. 36 y/o. 12 Aug. 1864, pupuria, Jarvis. M-922

RANSOM, MELVIN T. Co. B, 51st. Mass. 222 July 1863, typhoid, Camden St. M-640

RAPP, LEWIS Pvt. 28th. N.Y. Regt. 10 Jan. 1862. M-40

RAPP, THOMAS J. Co. H, 3rd. Pa. Art. 23 y/o. 19 Nov./Dec? 1863, "killed by falling off bank". Sent home

RATHBUN, JAMES L. Co.G, 8th. R. Island. 43 y/o. 30 Sept. 1862, anemia. M-341

RAWLINS, H.W. Co. K, 75th. Ohio. 36 y/o. 2 Sept. 1863, gunshot, Jarvis. M-719

RAWSON, DANIEL Co. K, 36th. Mass. 39 y/o. 7 Aug. 1863, gastro interitis, Patterson Park. M-610

RAY, WILLIAM Co. E, 112th. Ill. 20 y/o. 1 June 1864. M-805

REAMER, HENRY Co. I, 11th. Pa. 20 y/o. 14 July 1864, drowned. M-905

REASONER, HENRY M. Co. H, 7th. Mich. Cavl. 17 y/o. 31 July 1863, gangrene, Camden St. M-686

RECTOR, JAMES Co. H, 2nd. Tenn. 21 y/o. 23 May 1864, diarrhea. M-865

REDING, JOHN D. 5th. N.Y. Artl. 11 Aug. 1863, sunstroke, Camden St. M-679

REED, SAMUEL 45th. Ohio. 28 y/o. 7 May 1864, diarrhea, Patterson Park. M-838

REEDER, L. Co. L, 1st Pa. Cavl. 19 y/o. 11 Sept. 1862, McKim's. M-327

REEDEY, GEORGE 3rd. Mass. Cavl. 26 Oct. 1864, gunshot wound, National. M-1128

REILEY?, SYLVESTER Mc? 1 Nov. 1862, pneumonia. M-418

REIM/N?, FREDERICK A. Co. K, 1st. Pa. Res. 23 y/o. 1 Nov. 1862, peritonitis, Patterson Park. M-419

REINHARDT, FREDERICK Co. A, 105th. Pa. 20 y/o. 14 Jan. 1863, diptheria, Stewart's. M-542

REPPLOGEL, DANIEL Co. A, 61st. Pa. 28 y/o. 22 Sept. 1864, typhoid fever, Jarvis. M-1045

REYNOLDS, RAY T. Co. A, 18th. Mass. 20 y/o. 11 July 1862, typhoid, Nat. Hotel Hosp. M-209

REYNOLDS, RICHARD Co. E, 9th. Vt. 5 Jan. 1862. M-524

REYNOLDS, URIAH Co. H, 9th. Vermont. 20 y/o. 6 Jan. 186?, typhoid, Nat. Hotel. M-524

RICE, J.R. Co. H, 38th. Va. C.S.A. 39 y/o. 14 Jan. 1864, gunshot wound. V-37

RICH, CHARLES Co. E, 10th. Ohio. 20 y/o. 3 Sept. 1864, diarrhea, Patterson. M-990

RICHTER, CHARLES Co. K, 47th. Pa. 46 y/o. 2 Sept. 1864, diarrhea, Newton. M-989

RICHTER, GEO. Co. C, 7th. Ind. Vol. 24 Aug. 1863, Ft. Masters. M-714, sent home

RICKARDS, CHAS. H. 21 y/o. 4 June 1862, typhoid, Camden St. Hosp. M-153

RIKER, W.H. Co. G, 4th. N.Y. 25 y/o. 18 May 1862, gunshot, Nat. M-99

RISER, ALLEN C. Co. A, 1st. Va. Inf. 15 Feb. 1862, typhoid, U.S.A. Hosp., Camden St. M-55

RITTER, WM. Co. D, 61st. Ohio. 29 y/o. 23 Mar. 186?, pulmonalis, Continental. M-561

ROACHE, ALEX Co. A, 2nd. Pa. Cavl. 19 y/o. 23 May 1864. M-855

ROBBENS, SAML. Co. G, 16th. Maine. 28 Apr. 1864. M-788

ROBERTS, JACOB Co. A, 9th. Va. 29 y/o. 29 Aug. 1862, diarrhea, Camden St. M-987

ROBINS, PVT. Co. C, 4th. Wisc. Vol. 21 y/o. 18 Dec. 1861, rupture, Adam's House Hosp. M-21

ROBINSON, E.P. Sgt. Co. A, 149th. Ohio. 21 y/o. 8 July 1864, typhoid fever. Sent home

ROBINSON, FRANCES E. 100th. N.Y. 18 Sept. 1862. M-327

ROBINSON, JOHN Paroled prisoner. Co. E, 45th. Ky. 21 y/o. 22 Apr. 1864, typhoid & starvation, Jarvis. M-787

ROBINSON, JOHN Co. F, 27th. Conn. Vol. 18 June 1863, diarrhea, McKim's. M-602

ROBINSON, JOHN T. Co. A, 1st. Mass. 26 y/o. 17 July 1863, gunshot. M-659

ROBINSON, JOSEPH Co. H, 87th. N.Y. 26 Dec. 1862, contusion, West's. M-511

ROBINSON, JOSEPH Co. D, 101st. Pa. 1 June 1862. M-144

ROBINSON, SAMUEL Co. H, 10th. Mich. 10 May 1862. M-848

ROBINSON, THURSTON J. Co. ?T/Y, 20th. Maine. 20 y/o. 9 Nov. 1862, typhoid. Sent home.

ROBINSON, URIAH Co. L, 2nd. Pa. Cavl. 34 y/o. 8 Sept. 1864, gunshot, Camden St. M-992

ROBINSON, WESLEY Co. E, 6th. N.J. 25 y/o. 2 June 1862, "wounded at the battle of Williamsburg". M-146

ROGGE, DEDERICH Co. E, 46th. N.Y. 50 y/o. 19 Dec.(d. 14 Dec.)1862, dropsy. M-496

ROHN, PETER Co. C, 5th. Md. 24 Mar.(d. 20 Mar.)1862, consumption, Adams House. M-74

ROOD, RUFUS Co. H, 5th. Conn. Regt. 25 y/o. 27 Oct. 1861, typhoid, Nat, Hotel Hosp. M-2

ROONEY, JAMES Co. I, 87th. Pa. 24 Feb. 1864, Camden St. M-?6/744

ROSE, JAMES R. Co. ?D, 3rd. Md. Regt. 7 Nov. 1862, typhoid. M-429

ROSE, ROBERT 10th. Md. 18 y/o. 27 Mar. 1864, gunshot, Lafayette Barracks. M-779

ROSS, JAMES A. Co. A, 8th. Fla. CSA 18 July 1863, gunshot wound. V-40, grave #38

ROTTENBURG, AUGUSTUS Co. C, 1st. Md. 29 y/o. 26 Apr. 1862, typhoid. Res. Lewes/Lewis? M-358

ROWE, HEWS T. Co. K, 5th. N.C. C.S.A. 16 July 1863, "gunshot in head". V-40

ROWE, JOHN C. Co. B, 149th. Ohio 17 Aug. 1864, typhoid, Camden St. M-943

ROWELL, GEO. E. Co. H, 11th. N. Hampshire. 23 y/o. 10 Apr. 1964, pneumonia, Camden St. Sent home

RUCHE, ADOLPHUS Co. A, 13th. Pa. Cavl. 17 Nov. 1862. M-455

RUCKERD, JAMES Co. K, 2nd. Tenn. 24 Apr. 1864, diarrhea. M-833

RUNGAN, OGDAN H. Co. F, 30th. N.Y. 13 Mar. 1863, mania port., Nat. M-570

RUSSELL, CLARK H. Co. C, 11th. Vermont. 28 y/o. 28 Aug. 1864, gunshot wound, Camden St. M-965

RUSSELL, M.B. Co. B, 12th. S.C. C.S.A. 25 y/o. 31 July 1863. V-38

RUSSELL, THOS. Co. B, 82nd. N.Y. 20 Aug. 1863, Ft. Masters. M-709

RYAN, PATRICK Battery D, 5th. U.S. Artl. 23 y/o. 8 Nov. 1862, typhoid. M-432

SANDS, JAMES 13th. Pa. Cavl. 8 Sept. 1862, apoplexy. M-322

SAUL, JOHN Co. F?, 55th. Ohio. 32 y/o. 26 July 1862, diarrhea. M-246

SAUNDERS, GEORGE Co. D, 7th. N. Y. H. Artl. 39 y/o. 19 June 1864, gunshot. Camden St. M-1016, sent home by Mr. Macher

SAWYER, CHAS. G. Co. E, 141st. Pa. 28 Jan. 1863, West's. M-556

SAWYER, MOSES Co. F, 5th. U.S. Artl. 24 y/o. Unm. b. Vt. 12 Sept. 1862, typhoid. M-331

SAY, HENRY Co. B, 11th. Md. 16 y/o. 7 Sept. 1864, typhoid, Camden St. M-971

SCHAEFFER, JACOB Co. D, 13th. Pa. 27 y/o. 9 Mar. 1863, pulmonalis, Nat. M-569

SCHERER, AUGUSTUS C. Co. B, 47th. Pa. 24 y/o. 29 Oct. 1864, gunshot wound, Newton. M-1088

SCHNEIDER, CHRISTIAN Co. E, 3rd. Md. Regt. 11 Feb. 1862. M-41

SCHOOMAKER, W.H. Co. H, 5th. Wis. Regt. 23 y/o. 5 July 1862, typhoid, National Hotel. M-186

SCHRIPTURE?, LAFAYETTE Co. I, 96th. N. York. 30th. May 1862. M-136

SCITES, NICHOLAS Co. K, 10th. N.J. 29 y/o. 27 Oct. 1864, gunshot wound, Jarvis. M-1101

SCOTT, JOHN Confederate prisoner. 11 May 1862, "shot in the lungs". M-1

SCOTT, JOHN Co. K, 9th. N.Y.H. Artl. 47 y/o. 15 Sept. 1864, dysentery, Patterson. M-1002

SEARLE, JNO. E. Co. H, 3rd. Vt. Inf. 26 y/o. 25 July 1864, pyaemia? M-901

SEARS, JOSEPH Co. A, 5th. Pa. 3 Jan. 1862, National. M-525

SECOR, WM. H. Co. F, 9th. N.Y.H. Artl. 51 y/o. 3 July 1864, gunshot, McKims. M-909

SEISON, JAMES 19 June 1863, Newton. M-544

SELISS, FREDERICK Co. H, 151st. N.Y. 46 y/o. 864, dysentery, Jarvis. M-1076

SELLECK, SGT. 21 May 1862, National Hotel Hosp. M-99

SEPACK, HENRY Co. E, 4th. Ky. Cavl. 33 y/o. 22 May 1864, bronchitis. M-854

SHAFER, JOHN Co. B, 82nd. Ill. 30 y/o. 29 Nov. 1862, typhoid, National. M-449

SHAPLIN, JACOB Co. B, 23rd. Ill. 47 y/o. 27 Aug. 1864, gunshot wound, Jarvis. M-984

SHAUNTAN, SGT. M. Co. F, 12th. U.S. Artl. 3 Aug. 1862. M-273

SHAW, JOHN A. Co. D, 51st. N.C. C.S.A. 14 Oct. 1864, "brought dead to the hospital". V-?

SHAW, T.W. Co. H, 11th. Ala. C.S.A. 25 y/o. 3 Mar. 1864, gunshot wound, West's. V-37

SHAW, WILLIAM Co. K, 2nd. O.R.C. 20 y/o. 28 July 1862, sclop., Camden St. M-?

SHELL, JOHN Co. C, 6th. Mich. 21 y/o. 30 Dec.(d. 25 Dec.)1862, pulmonalis, Nat. Hotel. M-514

SHEPARD, MARTIN Co. F, 89th. N.Y. 26 y/o. 1 Dec. 1862 (?bur. 29 Nov.), typhoid. M-314

SHERICK, JOHN A. Co. E, 34th. Ohio. 30 y/o. 2 Oct. 1864, erysipelas, Jarvis. M-1053

SHERMAN, CHARLES Co. B, 8th. N.Y.H. Artl. 17 y/o. 27 June 1864, gunshot, Patterson. M-887

SHERMAN, JEFFERSON D. Co. B, 92nd. N.Y. 3 June 1862. M-147

SHERMAN, JOHN A. 81st. N. York. 15 Oct. 1862, West Buildings. M-383

SHERRY, GEO. "Substitute for Wm. E. Ross". 19 y/o. 19 Sept. 1864, "gunshot by guard while attempying to escape", Camden St. M-1016

SHERWOOD, GILBERT F. Co. K, 144th. N.York. 31 y/o. 22 Aug. 1863, diarrhea, Jarvis. M-712

SHERWOOD, ROBT. Co. F, 10th. N. Jersy. 20 y/o. 17 Sept. 1864, "gunshot wound right leg, Jarvis. M-1023

SHILLING, C.C. Co. B, 7th. Maine. 24 y/o. 4 Nov. 1861, congestion of lungs, Adams House Hosp. M-4, body #2

SHINNING, R.P. Co. B, 14th. Va. C.S.A, 14 Oct. 1864. V-?

SHIPMAN, MORRISON Co. H, 92nd. N.Y. 23 May 1862, Patterson Park Hosp. M-117

SHOEN, WILLIAM Co. E, 10th. V.R.C. 44 y/o. 30 July 1864, typhoid. M-898

SHOULDERS, JACOB Co. B, 15th. Va. 26 y/o. 13 Sept. 1864, typhoid fever, Jarvis. M-998

SHOWERS, H.B. Penn. Vol. 4 July 1862. M-183

SHREEVE, LEVI Co. K, 57th. Pa. 20 y/o. 1 June 1864, gunshot, Camden St. M-862

SHULTZ, FREDERICK Co. F, 49th. N.Y. 28 y/o. 24 May 1864, tetanus. M-866, sent home.

SHULTZE, FRED'K Co. C, 42nd. N.Y. 26 July 1863, gunshot, McKim's. M-637

SHUTE, A.R. Corp. Co. F, 12th. N.J. 22 y/o. 5 Aug. 1863, gunshot, Jarvis. M-673

SICKLES, N.B. Co. K, 154th. N. York. 19 y/o. 30 Dec. 1862, typhoid, National. M-515

SIMMS, J.C. Co. E, 5th. Wis. Vol. 32 y/o. 20 Sept. 1862, diarrhea, Newton Univ. M-332

SIMOND, H.B. 64th. N.Y. 1 Apr. 1862. M-77

SIMONDS, HENRY C. Co. C, 20th. Maine. 29 y/o. 18 Dec.(d. 14 Dec.) 1862, typhoid, Patterson Park. M-494

SIMPSON, DAVID F. Co. D, 20th. Maine. 23 y/o. 8 Dec. 1862, typhoid, National. M-457

SITES, GEO. Co. D, 81st. Pa. 29 y/o. 3 Jan. 1863, diarrhea, National. M-520

SKELMAN, I.E. Co. E, 17th. Pa. 17 y/o. 23 Sept. 1864. M-1028

SKIPPER, M. Co. D, 46th. N.C. C.S.A. 13 Oct. 1864. V_?

SLACK, THEODORE H. Co. D, 122nd. Ohio. 22 July 1863, typhoid. M-693

SLACK, WM. F. Co. C, 1st. Regt. Potomac Home Brigade. 16 y/o. 27 Dec. 1861, pneumonia. W/VV-42

SMALL, BENJ. F. Co. C, 7th. Pa. R.C. 21 y/o. 18 Feb. 1864, dropsy, Camden St. Sent home.

SMART, A.M. Co. K, 11th. N. Hampshire. 25 y/o. 7 Apr. 1863, typhoid, Nat. Hosp. Sent home by Mr. Macher.

SMITH, Son of DR. N.R. Removed from the South. 14 Nov. 1865. CC-24,26

SMITH, AND. Co. B, 151st. N.Y. 29 Nov. 1862. M-430, sent home.

SMITH, DAVID Co. I, P.R.C. 30 July 1862. M-254

SMITH, DAVID Co. F, 138th. Pa. 18 y/o. 25 Oct. 1862, gunshot wound, National. M-415

SMITH, DAVID J. Co. I/T?, 11th. N.C. C.S.A. 20 July 1863, gunshot wound. V-40

SMITH, ELIAS W. Co. D, 6th. New Hamp. 18 y/o. 31 Mar. 1863, diarrhea, Nat. M-447; "Body delivered to H.C. Murray."

SMITH, ELISHA M. Co. I, 20th. Mass. 14 July 1863. M-615, sent home.

SMITH, J.H. Co. K, 128th. N.Y.V. 9 Oct. 1862, hypertrophy of the heart, West's Hosp. M-379

SMITH, JACOB Co. C, 48th. Penn. 42 y/o. 3 May 1863, diarrhea, West Buildings. M-595

SMITH, JOHN F. Co. E, 12th. Iowa. 24 y/o. 18 Nov. 1862, pulmonalis, West building. M-435

SMITH, JONATHAN Co. B, 8th. Ohio. 20 y/o. 22 Sept. 1864, typhoid fever, Patterson Park. M-1026

SMITH, LEWIS 27th. Mich. S.S. 54 y/o. 1 Aug. 1864, dysentery & gunshot wound. M-914

SMITH, MOSES 16 July 1863, gunshot, Newton. M-651

SMITH, R.L. Co. B, 17th. U.S. Infantry. 27 July 1863, gunshot, Jarvis. M-666

SMITH, W.B. Co. A, 7th. Ga. C.S.A. 16 Oct. 1864. V-?

SMITH, WHEATON R. Co. I, 1st. Mich. 20 y/o. 3 Mar. 1864, pneumonia, Camden St. M-769

SMITH, WM. Co. C, 75th. La. 17 Oct. 1863, consumption, Patterson Park. ?-739

SNEDEKER, JOHN 5th. N.Y. Battery. 47 y/o. 2 Aug. 1862, dysentery. M-313

SNELL, RICHMOND Co. A, 114th. N.Y. 21 y/o. 15 Sept. 1862, typhoid, Nat. Hotel. M-338

SNIDER, WM. Co. M, 13th. Pa. Cavl. 19 y/o. 23 June 1864, diarrhea, Jarvis. M-154

SNOW, BARNEY Co. C, 3rd. Md. Cavl. 40 y/o. 24 Aug. 1863, brain, Jarvis. M-715

SNYDER, FINLEY Co. D, 38th. Wisc. 21 y/o. 13 May 1864, pneumonia, Camden St. M-846

SNYDER, WM. Co. K, 22nd. Iowa. 26 y/o. 22 Sept. 1864, dysentery, Patterson Park. M-1027

SOLLAND, FRANKLIN Co. E, 122nd. Ohio. 22 y/o. 19 Aug. 1864, typhoid, Jarvis. M-920

SPEER, THEO. C.S.A. 15 May 1862, gunshot. Vault.

SPENCER, J.A. Co. C, 145th. Pa. 19 y/o. 15 July 1863, gunshot wound, McKim's. M-656

SPENCER, JEREMIAH Co. J, 43rd. N.Y. 55 y/o. 8 Oct. 1863, general debility, Jarvis. M-736

SPORTEDER, CHARLES "Nurse at Camden St.". 25 y/o. 20 June 1864, gunshot, Camden St. M-875

SPRAGUE, JAMES Co. G, 1st. Mich. Cavl. 18 y/o. 3 Nov. 1861, measles, National Hospital. M-2, body #2.

SQUIRE, EDSON L. Co. K, 27th. N.Y. 18 May 1863, Camden St. Hosp. M-594

STAHL, JOHN Co. E, 123rd. Ohio. 19 y/o. 10 Sept. 1864, pneumonia, Jarvis. M-994

STAHL, WILLIAM Co. G, 93rd. Pa. Vol. 19 y/o. 27 Oct. 1864, typhoid, National. Sent home.

STANLEY, HEZEKIAH Co. K, 8th. Mich. 18 y/o. 8 May 1864, pulmonalis, Camden St. M-831

ST CLAIR, HENRY Co. D, 12th. Md. Milita. 16 y/o. 1 Aug. 1864, typhoid. M-900

STEEGAR, CHARLES H. Co. F, 98th. N.Y. Regt. 21 y/o. 10 July 1862. M-207

STEHLER, PHILIP Co. B, 49th. N.Y. 33 y/o. 5 Nov. 1862, typhoid, Nat. M-424

STEIGER, T.E. Miss. Regt. C.S.A. 21 Apr. 1864, "killed". V-?

STEINBERG, HENRY 14th. Regt. Excelsior Brigade. 9 July 1863. M-606

STENG, FREDERICK Co. F, 2nd. Del. 24 Dec. 1862, marasmus. M-499

STETTER, DAVID 89th. Vet. Res. Corps. 46 y/o. 20 Apr. 1864, pulmonalis, Camden St. M-963

STEVENS, EGBERT M. Co. C, 15th. Mass. 12 Feb. 1863, pulmonalis. M-491

STEVENS, JOHN Co. F, 30th. Maine. 34 y/o. 27 Aug. 1864, diarrhea, Jarvis. M-967

STEVENSON, S.M. Co. H, 5th. Texas C.S.A. 7 Aug. 1863, gunshot. V-38

STEVENSON, Saml. W. Co. E, 34th. Ohio. 26 y/o. 16 Aug. 1864, erysipelas, Jarvis. M-942

STEWART, DANIEL A. Co. H, 107th. N.Y. 23 y/o. 22 Sept. 1863, typhoid fever, Newton. Sent home.

STEWART, GEORGE H. Co. C/G?, 83rd. Pa. 26 y/o. 15 Aug. 1862, gunshot. M-303

STEWART, MARSHALL Co. G, 5th. Regt. N.Y. Artl. 31 July 1862. M-265

STHAL, JOHN "Soldier". 12 Nov. 1864. J-31

STICKNEY, ELON? Co. I, 92nd. N.Y. 1 June 1862. M-143

STILL, JAMES 72nd. N.Y. 17 y/o. 11 Mar. 1864, pneumonia, Camden St. M-775

STODDARD, CHARLES T. Co. K, 137th. N.Y. 22 y/o. 27 Dec.(d. 24 Dec.) 1862, typhoid, National. M-509

STODDARD, I.H. Co. L, 1st. Regt. Art., N.Y. Vol. 5 Mar. 1862. M-?

STODDARD, JOSIAH Co. K, 38th. Mass. 23 y/o. 22 Nov. 1862, typhoid, Stewart. Sent home.

STONE, G.W. Pvt. Co. A, 12th. Mass. 29 y/o. 23 ?Feb. 1863, gunshot, Nat. Hotel. M-575

STORY, WM. J. Pvt. Co. E, 11th. N.Y. 29 Sept. 1862. M-364?

STREET, BENJ. F. Co. K, 104th. Pa. 23 y/o. 26 July 1862, typhoid, National Hotel. M-248

STREETER, MARSHALL S. Co. F, 14th. N. Hamps. 22 y/o. 10 Oct. 1864, gunshot, National. M-930

STRICKLAND, GEO. Co. A, 9th. N.Y.H. Artl. 38 y/o. 12 July 1864, gunshot, Patterson. M-892

STRINGER, HY. Co. D, 29th. Penn. Regt. 23 y/o. 15 Dec. 1861, typhoid, Nat. Hotel Hosp. M-20

STRONG, LEVI Co. H, 83rd. Pa. 6 Aug. 1862. M-283

STRONG, PHILEMON B. Co. I, 15th. N.Y. Cavl. 33 y/o. 28 Sept. 1864, diarrhea, National. M-1036

STROUD, ANDREW Co. F, 13th. Ind. 30 y/o. 7 Feb. 1863, diarrhea, Calvert St. M-571

STUCKEY, JOHN 2nd. Maine. 19 Apr. 1864, "died on the boat from Old Point here, from starvation", West's. M-785

STURDEVANT, JAMES Co. I, 61st. N.Y. 3 June 1862. M-148

STURGIS, D.R. Co. G, 85th. Pa. 34 y/o. 29 May 1862, typhoid, National Hotel Hosp. M-133

SUDGATE, JOHN Co. F, 54th. Pa. 55 y/o. 17 May 1864, debilities. M-827

SULLIVAN, JOHN Co. D, 48th. Regt. Pa. 18 y/o. 13 Oct. 1862, vulnus schopt_ _, Newton Hosp. M-383

SULLIVAN, JOHN Co. C, 4th. Regt. Cavl. 30 y/o. 7 May 1864, diarrhea. M-824

SUTTON, JOHN Co. I, 55th. Ohio. 19 y/o. 17 July 1862, typhoid, National. M-226

SWARTZ, BENJAMIN Co. K, 131st. Ohio. 37 y/o. 20 Aug. 1864, typhoid, Camden St. M-956

SWEENY, PATRICK Co. G, 88th. Pa. Vol. 29 July 1862. M-256

SWEET, GEO. M. Co. F, 145th. Pa. 22 July 1863, gunshot, West's. M-644

SWIFT, RH'D. Co. H, 81st. Penn. 30 y/o. 2 July 1862, typhoid, National Hotel. M-181

TALON, MICHAEL Co. A, 7th. Maine. 23 Sept. 1862. M-350

TANNER, JOHN 28th. N.Y. 9 July 1862, National. M-201

TARIGH, JAMES Co. C, 1st. Mich. Cavl. 16 y/o. 27 Aug. 1864, gastric fever, Jarvis. M-963

TARR, SIMON Co. E, 20th. Maine. 8 Nov. 1862, dysentery. M-123, "removed and sent home".

TATE, WILIAM W. Co. C/G?, 76th. Pa. 28 y/o. 5 Dec. 1861, pneumonia, Adams House Gen. Hosp. M-13, body #2.

TATTAN?, JAMES F. 19 y/o. 4 Nov. 1862, dyptheria, Lexington St. Hosp. M-423

TAYLOR, ABRAHAM Co. B, 2nd. Del. 20 y/o. 20 July 1863, schoptimus, Newton. M-646

TAYLOR, CHARLES Co. F, 66th. N.C. Inf. C.S.A. 21 Oct. 1864. V-?

TAYLOR, GEORGE D. Co. C, 4th. Vt. 19 y/o. 19 Aug. 1862, typhoid, Newton University.

TAYLOR, JAMES Co. C, 50th. N.Y. 32 y/o. 24 Dec.(d. 20 Dec.)1862, diarrhea, Continental. M-500

TAYLOR, NATHAN Co. C, 13th. Vt. 16 July 1863. M-620

TENNANT, ALEX Co. C, 2nd. Md. 23 Apr. 1864, diarrhea, West's. M-798

TERMAIN, JOSEPH S. 18 y/o. 27 Oct. 1864, gunshot, Jarvis. M-1086

TERRILL, JOHN T. Sgt. Co. B, 39th. Ill. 28 y/o. 16 July 1864, pneumonia. M-904

TEXTON, ANTON Co. H, 26th. Wis. 42 y/o. 22 July 1863, gunshot, Jarvis. M-658

THAYER, ALBERT W. Co. K, 8th. Mich. 29 Mar. 1864, pneumonia, Camden St. M-781

THAYER, DANIEL K. Co. D, 4th. N.Y. Inf. 23 y/o. 19 Sept. 1864, gunshot, West's. M-1022

THOMAS, EDW. "Soldier". 8 Aug. 1862. M-290

THOMAS, GEO. A. Co. A, 7th. R.I. 29 y/o. 15 Apr. 1863, diarrhea, West's. Sent home.

THOMAS, HENRY Co. F, 69th. Pa. 16 July 1863. M-618

THOMAS, TERRENCE Co. E, 1st. Conn. Cavl. 23 y/o. 20 Aug. 1863, Jarvis. M-713

THOMPSON, EDWARD Pvt. 15th. N.Y. 17 yr., 23 d/o. 20 Dec. 1861, "injury of the brain". Removed home.

THOMPSON, ELIAS Co. F, 63rd. Regt N.Y. 15 June 1864, Camden St. M-873

THOMPSON, E.J? Co. G, 8th. Va. C.S.A. 32 y/o. 29 Aug? 1864, gunshot wound. V-36

THOMPSON, I/J? L. Co. C, 120th. N.Y. 20 y/o. 22 July 1863. M-647

THOMPSON, JAMES Co. H, 103rd. Pa. 26 June 1862. M-176

THOMPSON, JOHN A. Co. K, 25th. Ohio. 27 July 1863, West's. M-639

THOMPSON, JOHN E. Co. H, 85th. N.Y. 16 y/o. 9 June 1862, typhoid, National Hosp. M-154

THOMPSON, JOHN W. Co. B, 5th. Wis. 21 y/o. 10 Aug. 1864, typhoid. M-928

THOMPSON, SAMUEL Co. H, 49th. Pa. 35 y/o. 17 Sept. 1864, phthisis, Newton. M-1050

THOMPSON, SMITH Co. E, 16th. Ill. Cavl. 23 Apr. 1864, diarrhea, West's. M-812

THOMPSON, WM. Co. C, 96th. N.Y. 21 Apr. 1863, West's. M-585

THORNTON, H.F. Co. G, 72nd. N.Y. 12 Sept. 1862. M-330

THORNTON, PATRICK Co. J?, 57th. Mass. 31 y/o. 18 June 1864, gunshot, West's. M-878

TIGHE, PATRICK Co. G, 69th. N. Y. 21 Oct. 1862, drowned, Nat. M-403

TILLETTS, GEO. W. Co. L, 1st. Ct. Cavl. 28 y/o. 22 Feb. 1864, pneumonia, Jarvis. M-757

TILLY, JOHN B. Confederate soldier. On or after 7 June 1863. V-40

TILSON, E.F. 6th. Pa. R.C. 27 July 1862. M-249

TINDA, MARTIN Co. E, 7th. Wis. 37 y/o. 27 Mar. 1864, pneumonia, Camden St. M-783

TOLMAN, JOHN C. Co. C, 23rd. Mass. 23 y/o. 18 Sept. 1864, diarrhea, West's. M-1005

TOMLINSON, JAMES 5th. N.C. C.S.A. 17 May 1862, gunshot. Vault.

?TOWNSEND, A.C. 1st. U.S. Cavl. 21 July 1862. M-229

TRACEY, HENRY M. Co. B, 7th. N.Y. 18 y/o. 24 June 1864, gunshot, Patterson Park. M-880

TRACEY, JEREMIAH R. 10th. Md. 19 y/o. 6 Apr. 1864, pneumonia, Jarvis. M-808

TRACEY, ORRIN P. Co. H, 3rd. Pa. Artl. 29 y/o. 9 Apr. 1864, pneumonia, Jarvis. M-836

TRAHY, EDMUND Co. C, 73rd. N.Y. 22 y/o. 26 July 1863, gunshot, West's. M-667

?TRAIN/TRAVERS, DEXTER Co. A, 81st. N.Y. 21 May 1862. M-108

TRAINER, PATRICK Co. C, 3rd. Md. 12 Aug. 1862, heart. M-295

TRAY, N. Co. G, 2nd. Conn. Regt. 21 Oct. 1864. M-1095

TROWBRIDGE, H.H. Co. H, 55th. Ohio Vol. 20 y/o. 28 July 1862, typhoid, National Hotel. M-250

TRUITT, E.B. "Drafted man, Col. Belger's order". 5 Mar. 1863. M-567

TRUMPELMAN, OTTO 1st. Lt. Co. C, 119th. N.Y. 25 y/o. 26 July 1863, gunshot, Jarvis. M-694

TRYON, NATHAN Co. E, 4th. Ohio. 26 y/o. 10 Aug. 1864, gunshot wound. Sent home.

TULLY, THOS. Co. C, 12th. N. York. 23 y/o. 5 July 1862, typhoid, Nat. Hotel. M-189

TUPPER, FREDERICK Confederate soldier. 26 May 1865, gunshot. J-156

TURLINE, JOSEPH Co. H, 3rd. Reg. Inf. 20/30? y/o. 31 Oct. 1861, typhoid. M-3

TURNER, G.S. Co. I, 19th. Maine 18 y/o. 20 July 1863, gunshot, Jarvis. M-653

TURNER, HARRISON B. Co. D, 126th. Ohio. 38 y/o. 14 Oct. 1864, ?pyaemia, Jarvis. M-1066

TURNER, JAMES I. Co. B, 25th. Regt. 25 y/o. 25 Feb. 1864, inflamation, Lafayette Barracks. Sent home.

TURNER, J.P. Co. H, 24th. R. Mich. Vol. 29 y/o. 7 Sept. 1863, gangrene, Jarvis Hospital. M-728

TURNER, JOHN W. Co. B, 2nd. Conn. Art. 20 y/o. 19 Oct. 1864, diarrhea, Jarvis. M-1077

TURNEY, ISAAC Co. I, 3rd. Md. 21 y/o. 6 Oct. 1864, typhoid fever, Newton. M-1057

TWOMBLY, JOHN D. Co. D, 20th. Maine. 8 Nov. 1862, typhoid. M-431

TYES, J.M. Co. G, 6th. Ala. Inf. C.S.A. 26 Oct. 1864, diarrhea, West's. V-?

UNCAPHER, WM. H. Co. H, 140th. Pa. 26 y/o. 10 Aug. 1863, typhoid, Jarvis. M-680

UNKNOWN SOLDIER 2nd. Md. 18 Feb. 1862. M-65

UNKNOWN SOLDIER 28 Mar. 1863, "killed on the cars", Nat. Hosp. M-584

UNKNOWN SOLDIER Confederate Apr. 1863. M-39

UNKNOWNSOLDIER Confederate prisoner. On or before Apr. 1863. V-39

UNKNOWN SOLDIER Confederate. 11 May 1862, "shot". M-2

UNKNOWN SOLDIER 14 July 1863, "gunshot, unable to speak", West's. M-616

UNKNOWN SOLDIER Confederate. 15 July 1863. Union Relief. V-40

UNKNOWN SOLDIER Confederate. Apr. 1863. V-39

__, CYRUS Co. B, 111th. Pa. 17 July 1862, typhoid, Nat. Hotel. M-227

UNKNOWN SOLDIER 22 July 1862. M-233

UNKNOWN SOLDIER C.S.A. Recieved from Martinsburg. 27 Oct. 1864. V-?

UNKNOWN SOLDIER 18 Dec. 1865. V-?, Confederate Lot

UNKNOWN SOLDIER "Full particulars and description by Mr. J.H. Macher". 13 July 1862. Camden St. Hospital. M-220

UNKNOWN SOLDIER 1 Mar. 1864. Camden St. M-759

UNKNOWN SOLDIER 19 Mar. 1864. Camden St. M-777

UNKNOWN SOLDIER "Rebel prisoner d. at Union Relief Rooms". 14 July 1863. V-40

UNKNOWN SOLDIER Confederate prisoner. 20 July 1863, gunshot wound, unable to speak. V-40

UNKNOWN SOLDIER Co. K, 4th. Wis., Lt. Reynolds. 7 Feb. 1862. M-52

UNKNOWN SOLDIER "Has initials M.U. or M.W. on arm". 17 July 1863, National. V-655

UPTON, JOHN Co. K, 11th. Va. 18 y/o. 30 Aug. 1864, diarrhea, Patterson. M-988

USLEER, JOHN "Substitute". 28 y/o. 15 Aug. 1864, gunshot accident, Camden St. M-937

VAIL, DAVID Co. B, 6th. N.J. 22 y/o. 3 June 1862, "gunshot at Williamsburg", Nat. Hotel Hosp. M-151

VANDERSHIE_ _, AARON Co. E, 27th. Pa. 30 y/o. 21 Aug. 1863, gunshot, Camden St. M-710

VANKIRK, WM. J. Co. J, 2nd. Del. 21 y/o. 9 June 1864, measles, Camden St. M-860

V/BANNAKER, R_ _? Co. H, 104th. N.Y. 40 y/o. 27 Jan. 186, typhoid, West's. M-546

VAN SLACK, NATHAN 17th. Ind. Artil. 50? y/o. 23 Oct. 1862, vulnus sclopt., West's. M-412

VAN WALKER, A. Co. A, 7th. Wisc. 21 y/o. 22 Sept. 1863, gunshot, McKim's. M-665

VANWINKLE, HY. Co. E, 85th. N.York. 20 y/o. 30 Sept. 1862, diptheria. M-364

V/NARNEY?, JACOB W. Co. F, 161st. Ohio. 19 y/o. 4 Oct. 1864, typhoid fever, Patterson Park. M-1055

VENIER, JOHN Co. A, 9th. Md. 26 July 1863. M-633

VEST, WILLIS M. Co. C, 57th. Va. C.S.A. 21 y/o. 19 Aug. 1863, gunshot wound. V-38

VESTER, LEWIS Co. K, 6th. Mich. Cavl. 28 y/o. 26 Sept. 1864, diarrhea, Patterson Park. M-1042

VICE, GEORGE Co. E, 22nd. N.Y. Cavl. 17 y/o. 26 Oct. 1864. M-923

VON SCHMIDT, BERNHARDT Co. H, 10th. Md. 21 y/o. 24 Dec. 1863, typhoid fever. M-751

VOUGHT, WM. Co. F, 12th. Pa. Cavl. 20 y/o. 30 Sept. 1864, typhoid fever, Jarvis.

WACK, CHARLES Co. H, 5th. N.Y. 1 Dec. 1862(?bur. 29 Nov.)1862, typhoid. M-454

WADSWORTH, LUCIUS Co. F, 14th. Conn. 13 Sept. 1862, typhoid, Nat. Hotel Hosp. M-332

WAGNER, _ _ Co. D, 115th. Pa. 13 July 1863, Ft. Masters. M-617

WAGNER, B.C. Co. E, 9th. N.Y. 3 Jan. 1862, typhoid, Nat. Hotel Hosp. M-33

WAIT, ALBERT Co. G, 15th. Mass. 15 Oct. 1862, typhoid, West Buildings. M-393

WAIT, GRANVILLE Co. C, 30th. Maine. 37 y/o. 20 Aug. 1864, typhoid, Patterson Park. M-947

WALBURN, GEO. Co. A, 172nd. Pa. 39 y/o. 23 July 1863, diarrhea, Camden St. M-629

WALKER, CHARLES Co. K, 49th. Ga. C.S.A. 17 Oct. 1864. V-?

WALKER, JEREMIAH Co. F, 16th. Mich. 19 Nov. 1862, typhoid, Patterson Park. M-440

WALLACE, CHAS. S. Co. E, 18th. N.Y. 23 Sept. 1862, typhoid, Stewart's. M-348

WALLER, JAMES C. Co. C, 6th. Vt. 26 May 1862, typhoid, Camden St. Hosp. M-124 *Notation on opp. page-name might be Corp. Chas. C. Woollen.

WALSH, DAVID E. Co. E, 5th. Va. Cavl. 20 y/o. 29 Nov. 1863, "starved at Richmond", Union R. Rooms. M-666

WANDEL, ADAM Co. F, 75th. Pa. Vol. 56 y/o. 20 Nov. 1862, typhoid. M-386

WARD, JOHN Corp. Co. D, 3rd. Md. Cavl. 7 ?Nov./Dec. 1863, "shot", McDonald's. M-746

WARD, THOS. C. Co. Hosp. Steward. 28 y/o. 22 Sept. 1864, smallpox, 137 Fayette St. M-1050

WARFIELD, OWEN B. Co. H, 3rd. _.H.B. 25 y/o. 11 Aug. 1864, typhoid fever, Jarvis. M-920

WARNER, B. Co. H, 15th. N.C. 35 y/o. Sept. 1862, diarrhea, Nat. Hotel Hosp. V-42

WARNER, C. Co. D, 9th. Mass. 27 y/o. 21 June 1864, brain, West's. M-885

WARREN, WM. G. Co. E, 5th. Mass. Battery. 28 y/o. 11 Oct. 1862, National. M-392

WATTS, CHAS. H. Co. D, 8th. Md. 38 y/o. 18 June 1864, gunshot, Jarvis. M-876

WEAVER, PHILO. B. Co. K, 67th. Ohio. 20 y/o. 8 May 1864, starvation. M-830

WEBBER, JAMES R. Conf. soldier. 55 y/o. 16 Aug. 1865, consumption. "John H. W. paid Church Home". V-13

WEBSTER, GEO. Co. A, 4th. Md. 18 Dec. (d. 13 Dec.) 1862. M-498

WEED, ANDREW J. Co. H, 2nd. Va. Cavl. 22 y/o. 7 Aug. 1864. M-957

WEED, EDWIN Co. C, 141st. N.Y. 19 y/o. 11 Aug. 1863, typhoid, Camden St. M-678

WEEKLEY, GEORGE W. Co. A, 14th. Va. 19 y/o. 25 Sept. 1864, typhoid, Patterson. M-1044

WEEKS, AUGUSTUS Co. K, 111th. N.Y. 22 y/o. 22 July 1863, gunshot, Jarvis. M-627

WEIS, ANDREW Co. D, 3rd. Md. ?21/26 Aug. 1862, "disease contracted in the service". M-311

WEIT_ICK, GEORGE Co. F, 162nd. N.Y. 21 y/o. Sept. 1864, diarrhea, Patterson. M-972

WELCH, PETER Cpl. Co. G, 129th. N.Y. 3 Nov. 1862. M-420, sent home.

WELLER, JAMES C. C.S.A. 22 May 1862, gunshot, National Hotel. Vault.

WELLMAN, ALBERT Co. K, 24th. Maine. 13 Dec. 1862. M-479

WELSH, JOHN J. Co. B, 5th. N.Y. Artl. 24 y/o. 18 Mar. 1864, "wound", Jarvis. Sent home

WENGETT, W.H. Co. G, 7th. Pa. Cavl. 22 Oct. 1864, diarrhea, West's. V-?

WEST, WILLIAM 5th. U.S. Artl. 23 May 1862, typhoid, Nat. Hotel Hosp. M-114

WETCHER, NELSON Co. K, 1st. Mich. Cavl. 28 y/o. 7 Oct. 1864, diarrhea, Jarvis. M-1062

WHALEN, SAMUEL Co. B, 3rd. Md. Regt. 28 Jan. 1862. M-47

WHEAT, J.W. 19 May 1862, "died on the Steamer Vanderbilt". M-104

WHEELER, JAMES Co. B, 1st. N.Y. Artil. 24 y/o. 3 July 1864, gunshot, National. M-932

WHITE, DANIEL Co. G, 103rd. Pa. 18 y/o. 8 July 1862, phthisis. M-197

WHITE, EBAN Lt. Co. B, 7th. Md. Col'd..21 Oct. 1863, "shot", Camp Belger. Sent home.

WHITE, J.W. Co. F, 11th. N.C. C.S.A. 16 July 1863, "gunshot in lungs". M-40

WHITE, JAMES Co. A, 90th. N.Y. 27 Oct. 1864, gunshot wound, Patterson. Sent home.

WHITE, JOEL Co. F, 12th. U.S. Inf. 16 y/o. 16 Aug. 1862, gunshot, National. M-305

WHITE, JOHN S. Co. B, 45th. Ohio. 23 y/o. 9 June 1864. M-807

WHITE, PETER 13th. Pa. Cavl. 23 y/o. 16 Sept. 1863, killed on railroad, Union Relief. M-734

WHITE, SAMUEL Co. H, 3rd. Pa. Artl. 9 Oct. 1863, diarrhea, Patterson. M-737

WHITE, SILAS Co. C, 5th. N.Y. Artl. 18 y/o. 30 Dec. (d. 27 Dec.) 1862, epilepsy. Sent home.

WHITE, WILLIAM Co. E, 13th. Tenn. 28 Apr. 1864, diarrhea, West's. M-800

WHITING, GEO. A. Co. C, 5th. N.Y. Cavl. 25 y/o. 7 Oct. 1862, typhoid, Nat. Hosp.

WHITMAN, CHAS. Co. K, 1st. Ct. Cavl. 20 y/o. 28 Sept. 1864, diarrhea, Patterson Park. M-1047

WHITMAN, OLNEY A. Co. J, 7th. R. Island. 31 Mar. 1863, diarrhea, West's. Sent home.

WHITMAN, PHILIP Co. ?I/J, 13th. Va. 19 y/o. 30 Sept. 1864, typhoid, Patterson. M-1024

WIDERWAX, GEO. Co. K, 34th. Mass. 46 y/o. 31 Aug. 1864, catarrh, Patterson. M-938

WILEY, ALPHONSO Co. H, 31st. Maine. 19 y/o. 23 Apr. 1864, measles, Camden St. M-794

WILEY, NICHOLAS 2nd. P.R.C. 30 July 1862. M-263

WILLIAMS, EDGAR S. Co. I, 72nd. N.Y. 23 y/o. 27 Dec. (d. 24 Dec.) 1862, pulmonalis, Camden St. M-508

WILLIAMS, EZRA Co. E, 111th. Pa. 55 y/o. 18 Oct. 1862, chronic dysentery, Stewart's Mansion. M-399

WILLIAMS, GEO. Co. H, 36th. Mass. 27 y/o. 18 Apr. 1863, phthisis, West's. Sent home.

WILLIAMS, ?J./I. S. Co. D, 2nd. Md. Home Guards. 28 y/o. 14 Apr. 1862, ?mania, Camp Stewart. M-78

WILLIAMS, JAMES 47th. N.C. C.S.A. 7 Aug. 1863. V-38

WILLIAMS, MR. 24 y/o. ?23/28 Feb. 1863, Camden St. Hosp. G-single internment.

WILLIAMS, RICHARD Co. G, 9th. Mich. Cavl. 26 Apr. 1864, starved at Richmond. M-798

WILLIAMS, VALENTINE 6th. N.Y. Artl. 37 y/o. 1 July 1863, dropsy, Jarvis Gen. Hosp. M-603

WILLIAMSON, ROBT. Co. C, 81st. N.Y. 20 y/o. 13 July 1863, typhoid. M-212

WILLIAMSON, WM. R. Co. H, 2nd. N.Y. 5 June 1862, typhoid, Patterson Park. M-128

WILLIS, GEO. H. Co. B, 3rd. Md. Vols., Capt. Beckley. 9 Nov. 1861, "died at Camp Belger". M-6

WILSON, ALONZO T. Co. C, 10th. Maine. 17 y/o. 18 Feb. 1862, continued fever, Adams House. M-57

WILSON, S.A. Co. G, 8th. N.Y. Artl. 27 Jan. 1863, from Belger. M-555

WING, OLIVER Co. A, 8th. U.S. Infty. 22 y/o. 8 Oct. 1862, West Buildings. M-375

WINTERS, ANDREW J. Co. A, 150th. N.Y. 21 y/o. 16 Aug. 1863, typhoid fever, Newton. M-700

WISE, JOSEPH M. Co. B, 53rd. Ohio. 20 y/o. 1 June 1864, diarrhea. M-861

WOLF, JAMES Co. C, Purnell's 3rd. Inf. 49 y/o. 13 Nov. 1863, erysipelas. M-663

WONDER, N. Co. G, 141st. Pa. 31 July 1863, gunshot, McKim's. M-687

WOOD, ISAAC Co. F, 5th. Wisc. 18 Aug. 1862, typhoid. M-306

WOODRUFF, FRANKLIN B. Co. K, 147th. N.Y. 22 y/o. 3 June 1864, gunshot, Camden St. M-858

WOODSUNN, GEO. W. Co. A, 17th. Mass. Regt., Col. Amory. 28 y/o. 2 Dec. 1861, typhoid, "res. at Camp". M-28

WOODWARD, GEO. R. Co. B, 56th. N.Y. Vol. 34? y/o. 3 Oct. 1862, consumption. M-363

WOODWARD, HENRY B. Co. G, 7th. Mass. 14 June 1862, typhoid, Patterson Park Gen. Hosp. M-165

WOODWORTH, CHARLES C. Co. J, 11th. Vt. 18 y/o. 29 Aug. 1864, gunshot wound, Camden St. M-982

WOOLMAN, BENJAMIN Co. H, 13th. N.Y. 17 y/o. 3 Oct. 1864, West's. M-1054

WORDEN, ALEXANDER Co. C, 150th. N.Y. 21 y/o. 27 Aug. 1863, typhoid, Camden St. M-718

WRAY, HENRY Pvt. Co. B, 1st. Md. Cavl. 26 Oct. 1861, Adams House Hosp. M-1

WRIGHT, THOS. G. Co. B, 85th. Pa. Vol. 24 May 1862, typhoid, Nat. Hotel Hosp. M-119

WYLEY, DAVID D. Co. F, 25th. Mass. 41 y/o. 6 Oct. 1864, diarrhea, West's. M-1058

WYMAN, LEROY Co. A, 2nd. Vt. 20 y/o. 23 Oct. 1864, gunshot wound. M-1050/2

YANKSMITH, WENDELM Co. E, 151st. N. York. 30 y/o. 31 Aug. 1864, gunshot wound, Jarvis. M-979

YORK, ISAAC Co. A, 4th. Md. 3 Aug. 1863. O/S-1

YORK, MORRIS Co. E, 120th. N.Y. 20 y/o. 9 Aug. 1863, gunshot, Jarvis. M-622

YOUNG, AND. J. Co. D, 110th. N.Y. 29 y/o. 6 Dec. 1862, typhoid. M-461

YOUNG, GEO. H. Co. F, 56th. Mass. 26 y/o. 14 June 1864, gunshot, West's. M-860

www.ingramcontent.com/pod-product-compliance
Lightning Source LLC
Chambersburg PA
CBHW052104270326
41931CB00012B/2885

* 9 7 8 0 8 0 6 3 4 6 2 0 5 *